The most irresistible bags from the world's most unique stores

SHOPPING BAG SECRETS

By Sue Weiner & Fran Michelman

Photographs by Constance Brukin

AURUM PRESS

Acknowledgments

Our thanks to all the following without whom our shopping bags and all their secrets
would still be in our closets:

Charles Miers, Bonnie Eldon, Ellen Cohen, Charlotte Cousins at Universe Publishing;
and Christina Agnini, Brenda Anderson, Richard Behrman, Richard Buban, Ivan
Chermayeff, The Cooper-Hewitt Museum, John DiStephano, Franco Fava, Dorothy
Twining Globus, Belle Horwitz, Harrods Archives Department, Barbara Hawthorne,
Interstate Packaging, Kazuo Ito, Rita Jammet, Hiroji Kubota, Alex Lindsay, Virginia
Lohle, Nick Lyons, Joyce Mintzer, Carla Musanti, Parsons School of Design Library,
Angela Palladino, Lisa Rabidoux Finn, Patsy Rogers, Rita Rudner, Gerard Seradarian,
Susan Slover, Andy Warhol. To every fashion publication we could get our hands on.
To all the stores and designers who took the time to share their secrets with us. And, a
very special thanks to our mothers for setting us on the path toward the perfect little
blue bag and to Pat for putting up with our quest.

First published in Great Britain
1999 by Aurum Press Ltd
25 Bedford Avenue, London WC1B 3AT

A catalogue record for this book is available from the British Library.

ISBN 1 85410 618 X

10 9 8 7 6 5 4 3 2 1
2003 2002 2001 2000 1999

Design by Tony Palladino/Monica Fraile/Olga Lamm

Printed in Singapore

INTRODUCTION

They are on the streets of every major city in the world. They're also in closets. They're collected, coveted, shown off, stolen, recycled, displayed, auctioned, and given away. They're part of our everyday lives and our fantasies. They're three-dimensional, portable works of art, status symbols, and one of the most cost-effective advertising vehicles. Designed and illustrated by the world's finest commercial artists, they come in every shape, size, and color. They're the greatest freebies of all time. They're shopping bags.

This book is an homage to the shopping bag in all its glorious guises and the secrets they reveal about the most exciting places in the world and the people who carry them. The shopping bag has infiltrated every part of our lives, as the worlds of entertainment and consumerism blur with greater speed than a Concorde/Harrods sales special. No longer confined to department, specialty, and grocery

RITA JAMMET, CO-OWNER OF LA CARAVELLE.
PHOTO BY CONSTANCE BRUKIN

stores, the bag has moved into and out of restaurants, special events, political campaigns, performing arts, beauty salons, spas, museums, sports arenas, and virtually anything that can be wrapped.

Research for this book became a personal journey of discovery. The field work was diverse and unorthodox ranging from touring the shopping capitals of the world by foot to chasing people with uniquely fascinating bags down the street to talking to fellow collectors, shoppers, graphic designers, manufacturers, printers, distributors, retailers, museum curators, archivists, and anyone who found the subject as mesmerizing as we did. Friends and strangers opened their closets and collections, told us their stories, and

HISTORY

As soon as humans could gather, they invented containers to carry objects. It took just a little longer for the containers to become chic status symbols.

EARLY HISTORY

As early as Prehistoric times, people carried food and other possessions in a variety of containers: woven reed baskets, earthenware pots, and animal skins. Then came clay jugs, glass bottles, and leather bags. During the Middle Ages, people traveled great distances to buy goods in bulk so there was no great need for a carrier. But as cities and towns grew and people shopped more often and bought smaller amounts, wraps were needed.

In early sixteenth-century England, wallpaper was used for wrapping. Unsold manuscript pages were also used (an early form of recycling and a clever solution for remainder books).

FIRST BAGS

The first bags were made by twisting paper into cones and folding them at the bottom. By the mid-1800s, the industrial revolution made the mass production of paper feasible and printed paper was used for wrapping. The early bags were square and oblong in shape, with side, center, and bottom seams, and a pasted flat bottom inset. Later cord was attached through a pair of washers at each side of the bag, and handles were added.

BAND BOXES

One antecedent to the modern-day shopping bag was the band box—decorated oval boxes with a cover carried by both men and women and all classes. While the original boxes were used to transport the traveler's lightweight linen accessories, later they were filled with small purchases. The boxes were made out of cardboard and covered with wallpaper. Later papers were made especially offered a network of contacts. By the end of our whirlwind tour, we realized that we were only at the beginning. Enclosed between these covers is just a taste of the irresistible bags and places we found.

The process was a visual minefield of decisions. What bags to put in? What bags to leave out? How to categorize? We easily had enough bags in our collection for several volumes and great effort was made to narrow down the final selection to a number that would fit on these pages.

Although the key to our criteria will be found as you read the book. it is safe to assume that what these bags have in common is they are all must-haves for the closet or the street. As you will see in the opening chapter, "Designer Bags," we live in a time when the designers dictate style and have become household names. If you can't afford the clothes, then buy the perfume or the cosmetics and get the bag. While most of these lavish bags may not be made out of recyclable materials, they are recyclable by virtue of their beauty and longevity. They are made to last longer than this year's fashion and to be used repeatedly: a well-produced bag can be used 50 to 100 times. promoting the master's name and brand.

All of these bags have more in common than four sides and two handles. There are the black bags that are almost as prevalent as the little black dress: Barneys. Dolce & Gabbana. Sonia Rykiel. and the Empress of them all—the shiny black Chanel bag. There are the trendsetters with geometric cut-out shapes like Krizia and Felissimo: the "separated-at-birth" bags so alike except for the direction of their stripes Henri Bendel. Joseph. and Anya Hindmarch: the subtle off-white bags by the Italian master Armani and the all-American Calvin Klein who share the same camaraderie as their clothes

BANDBOX DEPICTING A WOMAN IN A CHARIOT DRAWN BY TWO GRIFFINS. UNITED STATES, c. 1839.
BLOCK-PRINTED PAPER ON CARDBOARD. 17 ½ x 14 x 13". COOPER-HEWITT, NATIONAL DESIGN MUSEUM,
SMITHSONIAN INSTITUTION/ART RESOURCE, NY. PHOTO COOPER-HEWITT, NATIONAL DESIGN MUSEUM,
SMITHSONIAN INSTITUTION/ART RESOURCE, NY. PHOTO BY DENNIS COWLEY

for this purpose and production of these boxes became a thriving cottage industry. Like the future shopping bag, band boxes were covered with all sorts of images. And like today's bags, the images were often advertisements for products, special events (the building of the Erie Canal), and political campaigns.

INVENTORS OF THE FIRST BAG
(of which there are several)

Herbert Kurz claims to have produced the first true carrier bag in 1906 (*Novum*, September 1996). It was the kind of brown paper bag still used in grocery stores today. Kurz entered his paper carrier in the list of registered designs under the catchy name "handfrei" (free-hand).

Meanwhile, Interstate Packaging claims to have invented in 1907 the first paper bag with cord handles that wrapped all the way around the bottom of the bag and that was attached with staples. These bags were assem-

INTRODUCTION (CONT.)

sometimes do: the transparent bags from Century 21 and Moss to the dreamy cloud scene on the Louvre museum's bag: the chic whites of Dior, Versace, and even one by Chanel: the lush home style bags from the handsomely illustrated MacKenzie-Childs to ABC Carpet & Home: the boldly graphic bags like Fauchon, Gap, MoMA, the Metropolitan Museum of Art, and Diptyque: the equally brazen colored bags from Christian Lacroix, Voyage, Pink, and Sentou Galerie: the unusually shaped bags from Valentino, to the Mulberry home bag, to the one-and-only Takashimaya: the black-and-white photo-driven bags of Kenneth Cole and Guess?, which perfectly contrast the whispering elegance of the Chloé and Hervé Leger masterpieces.

Then there are the bags that are so original, so different, that the only commonality is their uniqueness—the Moschino bag which practically giggles: the pastel, scal-

ANDY WARHOL'S CAMPBELL SOUP
SHOPPING BAG.
PHOTO BY BARBARA HAWTHORNE

loped Inès de la Fressange bags, which could easily move to Versailles: the sturdy, stable Hermès bag: the camouflage forest of Jean-Paul Gaultier: the ultramodern electric blue Yohji Yamamoto: the impetuous Yellow Rat Bastard: the flirty Victoria's Secret: the trendsetting colette: the rich Judith Leiber: and that very special little blue bag—and our number one—Tiffany's.

As diverse as the bags, so are the collectors we met along the way. From the shopper who hoards bags as mementos: to the Sotheby's commissionaire whose private collection is as sacred as religion: to La Caravelle's co-owner whose favorite bags are displayed on shelves and are the talk of her clientele: to a

bled entirely by hand and the decoration was pasted to the front. By 1927, Interstate improved the process to the point where images and text could be mechanically printed directly on the bag and, by 1936, the first fully automated machine to make the bag was invented.

Yet another contender to the title is Walter Henry Deubner, a grocer from St. Paul, Minnesota, who tried to come up with a method for his customers to purchase and carry home more goods. In 1919 he got a patent for the bag and a year later he had sold nearly a million bags. In 1934 he got a second patent for the first fully produced shopping bag.

CHANGES

Over the years, the bag has continued to improve. According to Alex Lindsay, of ModernArts Packaging, Inc., "major changes from the '50s and '60s have given

way to custom logotypes as an integral element in the bag design." During the '70s there was a significant breakthrough in printing, enabling shopping bags to precisely match any print advertising campaign. Joyce Mintzer of S. Posner Sons, Inc., also believes that today's technological advances have made it possible for the "creative possibilities to more than equal the functional."

Seymour Chwast, graphic designer and director of Pushpin Studios, agrees that "shopping bags are throwaway art," using Andy Warhol's famous Campbell Soup shopping bag as the perfect example. "Warhol began by taking an object that is normally discarded—the soup can—and created art from it. He took the idea to its logical extension by transferring the art back to a throwaway object—the shopping bag."

We agree in principle, but we would never throw away the bag.

Virginia woman whose home interior has been redesigned specifically to display her prize collection.

It was the revolutionary graphic design decade of the '60s that brought art together with everyday objects—T-shirts, mugs, matchbooks, record album covers, buses, subways and, of course, shopping bags. The Pop Art movement, combined with the sophistication of the production process and greater materials available, drew renowned artists to the medium, such as Roy Lichtenstein, Frank Stella, Salvador Dali, and Andy Warhol and his Campbell Soup shopping bag created for the exhibition "Supermarket Show." (A signed Warhol bag was recently auctioned for more than four thousand dollars at Sotheby's.) Major department stores such as Bloomingdale's and Harrods chose leading artists to create special bags for their in-store promotions, and museums realized that not only could they sell exhibition-related objects at the museum

gift shops, but they could offer beautiful bags for shoppers to take home with their purchases. One of the greatest portable message billboards of all time took off. Shopping bags and their collectors have not been the same since.

And neither have the streets of the world's major cities, where the shopping bag is an integral part of the visual buzz. Just one glance and you can discover all you need to know about a place and its shoppers. A second look demonstrates how the world has become one big global shopping market. When you read this book we are confident you will discover what we did—that the thrill of shopping is in the bag.

Sources: *Bandboxes and Shopping Bags: In the Collection of the Cooper-Hewitt Museum, The Smithsonian Institution's National Museum of Design* (Cooper-Hewitt exhib. cat., 1978); "The Paper Shopping Bag" (Interstate Packaging Corporation's general history); Radice, Judi, and Jackie Comerford. *Best of Shopping Bag Design.* Glen Cove, NY: PBC International, 1987; Wagner, Stephen C., and Michael L. Closen. *The Shopping Bag; Portable Art.* New York: Crown, 1986; Wright, Milton. "Successful Inventors." *Scientific American XI,* November, 1927.

BANDBOX DEPICTING AN ADVERTISEMENT. PRODUCED BY PUTNAM AND ROFF PAPER HANGINGS AND BANDBOX MANUFACTURER, HARTFORD, CT, 1823–24. BLOCK-PRINTED PAPER ON CARDBOARD. 17¾ x 13 x 12". COOPER-HEWITT, NATIONAL DESIGN MUSEUM, SMITHSONIAN INSTITUTION/ART RESOURCE, NY. GIFT OF MRS. FREDERICK THOMPSON, 1913-45-10A,B. PHOTO: COOPER-HEWITT, NATIONAL DESIGN MUSEUM, SMITHSONIAN INSTITUTION/ART RESOURCE, NY. PHOTO BY DENNIS COWLEY

When it comes to favorites, both sentimental and monumental,
we went to the experts (ourselves and others) for the best choices.

Here are THE BAGS TO KILL FOR

Best Color	Christian Lacroix
Most Outrageous Shape	Takashimaya
Best Handle	Hervé Leger
Best Logo	Fauchon
Most Adorable	Inès de la Fressange
Greatest Expectation	Tiffany & Co.
Best Original Design	Krizia
Best Traffic Stopper	Yellow Rat Bastard
Most Extraordinarily Ordinary	Bloomingdale's (Brown bag)
Most Extraordinary	Takashimaya (Japan)
Held Closest to Heart	Tiffany & Co.
Most Often Seen on the Street	McDonald's
Most Elegant	Givenchy
Most Casually Chic	GAP
Most Conservative Chic with a Twist	Paul Smith
Most Sexy	Victoria's Secret
Most Humorous	Moschino
Hardest to Part with	Christie's (Dresses bag)
Favorite Clones	Henri Bendel and Joseph
Carries Heaviest Load	Century 21
Most Prestigious	The white Chanel
Most Patriotic	Jerry's
Most Nostalgic	Bonwit's
Good Enough to Eat	La Marquise de Sévigné
Most Whimsical	Serendipity
Most Old World	Mariage Frères
Most Revolutionary	Commes des Garçons

Most Joie de Vivre	Octopus
Most Sophisticated	Louis Vuitton
Most Impressionistic	Jean-Paul Gaultier
Best Lamination	Fendi
Most Scenic	DKNY
Best History	Hermès
Best Transparent	Martine Sitbon
Most Computer Literate	Fogal
Most Recognizable	Harrods
Most Trendy	colette
Best Illustration	MacKenzie & Childs
Best Everyday Black	Barneys
Most Deceptive	Pink
Best Texture	Yohji Yamamoto
Most Curvaceous	Thierry Mugler
Most Flirty	Chloé
Most Subtle	Harry Winston
Most Heavenly	Versace
Most Hellish	Prada and Miu Miu for not being part of this book (We love the Miu Miu bag too!)

WHAT'S YOUR FAVORITE BAG?

"Barneys—because it has an austere chic, a touch of Japanese Zen aesthetics, and for a Londoner, a New York shopping bag has a hint of international jet-setting which is irresistible. The Bloomie's bag with its tough brown paper and sturdy handles has a certain democratic insouciance, whilst for real insider swank a small cream-and-black Jo Malone bag (carrying, of course the ginger and nutmeg oils) is hard to beat."
Lucia van der Post, Editor, "How to Spend It," *Financial Times*

"My favorite shopping bag is the generic 'mama' shopping bag that welcomes all of the 'baby' shopping bags that I've collected on a successful day of healthy consumerism. Sometimes my 'mama' bag isn't strong enough to hold all of her babies and she delivers them caesarian style in the middle of the street. I hate that." Rita Rudner, actress/comedienne

"My favorite bags come from Takashimaya in New York and second, Miu Miu in Milan."
Martha Nelson, Managing Editor, *InStyle*

Chapter 1
DESIGNER BAGS

THIS IS THE AGE OF DESIGNERS.
NO LONGER JUST STYLISH NAMES.
THEY ARE THREE-DIMENSIONAL, OFTEN MEDIA-CRAZED CELEBRITIES
WHO ARE SAVVY ENOUGH TO KNOW THAT THEY ARE DESIGNING
MORE THAN CLOTHES AND PERFUME—
THEY ARE SELLING DREAMS.
THE ESSENCE OF THEIR DREAMWORLD IS ALL IN THESE DESIGNER BAGS.

"I am a *fashionista* and proud of it. I adore fashion. I like to wear outrageous clothes.
to make an entrance. I think every woman should do something to catch the eye in the room."
Donatella Versace, *InStyle*, 1998
Carrying the bag works for us.

Chanel

The bag and the store are in a class by themselves. Gabrielle Coco Chanel, the woman behind the little black dress, the braided suit, the quilted bag, and the two-toned shoes was a designer's designer. When Karl Lagerfeld came along, he added his genius and revived and reinvented what was already there. Women everywhere still yearn for the perfect quilted handbag. But the real cachet is in having the special white carrier bag Coco designed only for her Paris store. We think it's worth the trip.

If it doesn't have a Chanel boutique, it's not a shopping capital.

Versace Boutique

One look at the new Versace bag and you just know Gianni went to heaven. It's a sumptuous, solid, pure white paper with the gold foil of an angel's halo. Not to mention the white cord handles that could decorate the pearly gates. Yet his clothes were anything but angelic. With his sister Donatella as his muse, his clothes screamed sex. And even without him, she's moving the company into the millennium brilliantly as one of the top-ten moneymakers. Even so, this bag is not free. No amount of pleading can cajole a salesperson to part with one. But it's worth a purchase. If you can't afford the couture clothes or accessories, go for the perfume or, even better, bold Versace paint for the lips in a container fit for a Chanel bag.

Versace Boutiques proliferate everywhere. Versace Jeans Couture, Versace Sport, Young Versace, Versace Intensive, Versus and Isante can be found in upscale malls and department stores.

"Chanel copied everything she did and made it commercial. But this is genius, no?" Karl Lagerfeld, designer for Chanel.

"I'm not interested in any work done for the masses." Gabrielle Coco Chanel, *Harper's Bazaar*, 1923

Chanel No. 5 was the first "designer" perfume. Still the perfect way to get one of those small Chanel bags.

"The goal is to have 100 CK Calvin Klein stores operating in Europe and the Mideast by the year 2001."
Gabriella Forte, Klein's president, *W*, 1997

Calvin Klein

It took a boy from the Bronx to challenge the reign of French and Italian supremacy in fashion by taking the haute out of couture and become better known than all the competition put together. But it was his jean line that brought him true superstar status by giving the masses the chance to wear designer clothing without the astronomical designer price tag. The world of fashion would never look or feel the same once Calvin Klein stamped his name on his first pair of jeans. That was until he tackled the underworld of underwear. The designer whose ads thrived on controversy (Brooke Shields, age 15, and "What comes between me and my Calvins? Nothing." to the full-sexed underwear ads with Marky Mark), Klein conquered middle America and is now preparing a full-scale global blitz. His stores are as streamlined and classic as his clothes, his Home Collection, and his shopping bag. In a world of black, Calvin Klein is soft white and beige. His shopping bag will be a passport to any country.

Soon to be everywhere.

Daryl K

Born in Ireland, Daryl Kerrigan is a true New Yorker—with her fashion roots nurtured by streetwear, thrift shops, and road trips across America. She made her mark with her first store in NYC's East Village, but it was her unisex, hip-hugging jeans that set her apart from everyone else and is what is most likely being carried in this bag.

Two stores in New York, one in Tokyo.

"Next Donna Karan."
The New York Times

Daryl K

21 Bond Street NYC

"I work as if I'm still in my grandmother's attic dressing up.
Clothes aren't everything. . . .
Clothes should make you feel happy,
relaxed, and ready to tackle any problems." **Agnès B.**

"A bag is a bag is a bag." Gertrude Stein

Marie Mercié

While you may need attitude to wear these hats, it is a must to stop by the store to see these works of art for the head. More elegant than a French patisserie, the hats are posed and poised for complete view. They define the word divine. Marie Mercié, former journalist and painter, says that when she's creating hats she "imagines a beautiful woman with panache, who would have fought in the Résistance." While her most stylish hats have no place in today's world of street fashion, one feels a little better just knowing they are there, just in case you can invent the right occasion to fit the hat. Catherine Deneuve, Shirley Maclaine and Faye Dunaway can.

One store in Paris.

agnès b.

From the woman who says she does not like fashion but likes clothes, agnès b.'s clothes have always had fashionable appeal. Note that the entire cast of *Pulp Fiction* was dressed in agnès b. attire. The look is French and simple and is meant for the modern, working woman who can also outfit her man and kids (from infant up). In fact, it's an Audrey Hepburn look for real people. The bag is just as strikingly simple, white with a black logo. But the true star is the carrier bag for children—which wears its red heart only.

Over 100 stores worldwide including Paris, London, and New York.

"The Partners have adopted Tanner Krolle's signature symbol of a circle in a square. which appears on the handbags. for the range of printed materials. The use of this device links the product with the brand identity in a seamless continuity."
Jess Harris. designer

Christian Dior/Baby Dior

In 1947 Christian Dior's "New Look" changed the face of fashion forever while causing riots in the streets of Paris. Dior died a decade later and has since been succeeded by Yves Saint Laurent, Marc Bohan, and Gianfranco Ferré. And now, John Galliano, who is destined to create Dior's new "New Look." The bag is as classic as Christian Dior. Baby Dior is even better. Get them hooked young.

Wherever the smart set is. →

Tanner Krolle

Declared by *Vogue* as "the next bag thing," even Cherie Blair carries one. So Prada and Gucci better watch out because Tanner Krolle has reinvented itself from the best-kept secret of the conservative wealthy. Founded as a saddler company 140 years ago, Krolle specializes in the kind of luggage that could easily last several lifetimes. Realizing that 70 percent of the leather goods business is in the handbag market, the company quickly developed a line of bags combining its reputation for quality with design aimed at the women who buy 5.2 bags a year. Krolle understands a woman and her relationship with her handbag: it's personal, it's a friend, she can never have too many, and she doesn't have to go on a diet to buy one.

London.

*"These are not bags for people who go to the gym.
They are for romantic vegetarians."*

Stella McCartney in *W* (1997) when asked about her handbags made to hold the Chloé girl's essentials: cell phone and keys.

Chloé

Genny/Byblos

A "Made in Italy" success story. So are the bags. Designed to be "extremely simple, sober, elegant, and practical," the bags mirror Genny's current designer, Rebecca Moses. But behind the Genny bag is a hotbed of associations with some of the most exciting designers. From the trendy Complice lines with Claude Montana and Dolce & Gabbana to Byblos's Keith Variety/ Alan Cleaver, and Richard Tyler, Byblos now has VH1's 1998 hottest new designer—John Bartlett—at the helm. Genny believes in talent.

Milan, Rome, Dubai, Jakarta, Kuwait, Tokyo, Nagoya, Osaka, Seoul.

Chloé

French Chloé, first to conceive "prêt-à-porter de luxe" when founded in 1952, has been reborn young, hip and thoroughly British. "I know what a chick wants," says the 26-year-old Stella McCartney, whose mother wore flowy Chloé in the '70s. "There's no street fashion in Paris. I don't walk down the street and think that chick's got a good little mixture."(*Harper's Bazaar*, 1997). Yet she's managed to come up with a perfect mixture: feminine fragility and sexy trash. While we can't imagine anything more beautiful than the current silky, peach Chloé bag, we hear Stella can. And we can't wait to see her new design. Stella, the ultimate "bag chick," says that if she finds a great bag she is happy all day, and we expect an equally chic shopping bag from her.

A remodeled boutique on Paris's Faubourg Saint-Honoré, others in Barcelona, Tokyo, Osaka, Singapore, Tapei, Hong Kong, and many more to come.

"Shopping bags are a girl's best friend. . . ."
sang Marilyn Monroe

Design: Adelaide Astori, prominent Italian graphic designer

"When something is out of place, you think maybe this woman has been in bed with someone. And that's good."

Rosella Tarabini, Molinari's daughter and design partner, *In Style*, 1998

Krizia

One of Italy's most innovative design houses went back to the classics when it named itself after Plato's dialogue *Critias*, in which the protagonist was a man unable to stop himself from giving women expensive jewels and dresses. (Where is he now?) The first Italian company to introduce prêt-à-porter, Krizia even managed to outlive its notoriety for inventing "hot pants." The bag with its see-through hole in the middle and silver-embossed logo is just as innovative and should be a classic.

Fifty-four stores worldwide.

Anna Molinari

The store's decor is even better than this coveted bag. Walk through the entrance under giant-size mosaic mannequin legs and find some of the sexiest clothes around. Adored by fashionites, this Italian designer knows how to dress a teen, appeal to a woman, and please a man. She and her daughter are set to conquer America.

Milan, Bari, London, Lisbon, Vienna, Singapore, Seoul, Taipei, Osaka, Tokyo, Jakarta, and Hong Kong.

"We like to redesign the bags every six months or so
to be eye-catching,
fun and season-appropriate."
Todd Oldham, public relations

"I want to be a shopping bag."
Andy Warhol

Todd Oldham

He's the Texan ringmaster of the MTV generation's school of style. He's all about fun, yet he's a family man too. He made his mom the president of his company. He's the ultimate in downtown New York style—his only store is in Soho. But, if you are looking for black, go elsewhere. He's cutting edge with color. Best known for his mosaic tile dress (rumored to have more than 1,700 colors and encompass the entire Pantone color chart), his bags are just as bold and brash. But you have to get there at least once a season to catch the latest. The one thing that does stay constant is his crown motif—as well it should, since he's the crown prince of downtown hip. His followers are equally legendary and loyal; when Cindy Crawford stopped cruising the catwalk, she still strutted for her friend Todd. He also made a guest appearance on the TV sitcom *The Nanny* as cousin Toddy. On and off the screen, his "cousin" Fran Drescher wears his clothes perfectly.

New York's Soho.

Comme des Garçons

Rei Kawakubo is a revolutionary. As with most revolutionaries, it's been reported that she has never cracked a smile. Who would have the time? After 25 years in business, she produces 11 lines, sells in 33 countries, has 389 stores in Japan alone and, then, creates new fabrics for every collection and never reuses them. Unlike the bag, which is sturdy, subtle, and with reinforced coated twined handles, and highly reusable. It's so good, it's revolutionary.

Wherever there's a clothing revolution.

To counteract all the outrageousness he had seen on recent runways.
Armani let his preferences be known
at the beginning of a recent collection.
"No plastique!" the master declared.
Which is fine with us. We're happy with our perfect little paper bag.

Giorgio Armani

The Italian word for style is spelled: G-I-O-R-G-I-O A-R-M-A-N-I. Pure and simple as his clothes, he is the master of understated luxury. The moment Richard Gere strutted across the screen in *American Gigolo*, women fell under the Armani spell. But it was as a womenswear designer that his name began to be spoken in the hushed tones reserved for religious experiences. And the truth is that Armani devotees feel his clothing is a religion—minimal, no fuss, black, muted, simple, pure. The kind of clothes you can wear straight from the office to the Academy Awards. Legend has it that Signor Armani does not allow fashion editors to mix his clothing with any others in fashion layouts. Who'd want to? Armani is a full-page statement of life—with the perfect bag to carry it off in.

Sixty Giorgio Armani Boutiques worldwide. Not to mention Emporio Armani and Armani Exchange. Currently expanded into lifestyle.

Ivana

Ivana Trump—everyone's favorite divorcée and the woman who proved that revenge against her ex-husband Donald is the fastest way to success. Ivana left the Plaza Hotel and opened her own House of Ivana, selling everything from fashion to perfume, in department stores and on TV shopping networks. When asked about her favorite shopping bag, Ivana replied: "I must confess, ever since I created the House of Ivana, and then its luxurious shopping bag, I don't use anyone else's! . . I love giving gifts in my bags, and I always keep a supply around the house because people are always asking for them."

Anywhere Donald isn't. →

"The more shopping bags a person is ashamed of,
the more respectable one is."
George Bernard Shaw

Cerruti 1881

Miami Vice. *The Hit Man*. Richard Gere in *Pretty Woman*. Michael Douglas in *Fatal Attraction*. Jeremy Irons in *Reversal of Fortune*. Nino Cerruti has his label on them all. From a family of weavers, his motto is "It's about seduction, not sex." How can he lose? Well, he did lose Giorgio Armani, who designed his first womenswear line for seven years, and, most recently, Narciso Rodriguez. But the shopping bag, like Cerruti, keeps on seducing.

Almost everywhere.

Laurel

Laurel, like its bag, is the more understated end of the business, aimed at the young businesswoman.

Ditto.

Escada

This German company is the largest purchaser of luxury fabrics in the world. It has built its megasuccess on computer design and sales technology. Todd Oldham is now the creative consultant. "Shrinking violets walk on by," says the *London Fashion Guide*. It's flashy, glittery, colorful womenswear. Why is the bag so conservative, Todd?

Ditto.

Moschino

Just like the bag, you can hang a smile on it. This is a design label with a sense of humor, just like the late Moschino and his utterly original designs. But there's no subtlety here. Words on dresses, safety pins, hearts everywhere (even on sleeves), Franco's legend lives on.

Wherever girls go to have fun. →

"People tell me that my humour is very un-Italian." Moschino once remarked. "And I take it as a compliment."

Jean-Paul Gaultier

To call him the enfant terrible of French fashion would be a cliché. But he and his bag certainly are not. It's the most elegant impressionistic version of street-smart camouflage-wear and it describes JPG to a tee. And, after all these years, he had his first haute couture collection in 1997, bringing together his uni-world, unisex, ethnic influences and his undeniable design brilliance. Vive le Gaultier.

One store in Paris.

Gucci

As trendy as bell-bottoms were in the '60s, so was Gucci. Both have reemerged as style-setters for the '90s. It's the bag to have, no matter what the contents and no matter where you get it—New York, Paris, London, Berlin, Hong Kong, or even Milan, thanks to that American classic, Ford (Tom that is). In fact, one of the first things he did in 1995 was to banish the classic green bag and put the G logo everywhere except on the new sleek bag. That went along with his philosophy in clothing—no underwear, no lines. Ah, but now he's designed an underwear line.

In all the world's major shopping capitals, where the store design makes as much of a statement as the bag—the newest one in Beverly Hills is raised from the sidewalk to look as if it's floating on air.

"We have everyone's attention, now the key is to dress them." Tom Ford, *W*, 1998

"Gucci has become me and I have become Gucci. We've merged." Tom Ford

"Any color you like, as long as it's black."
Thomas Ford, (father of the model-T Ford. Are you sure there's no relation??)

"He's more famous in Japan
than Michael Jackson." *Vogue*, 1998

Fendi

This is one of the "richest" shopping bags around. Laminated yellow/gold, embossed with the only initial many people ever need. But if you want to carry something that lasts a bit longer (devotees swear Fendis last a lifetime), their logoed leather is an art form. Along with luxury leather goods, this venerable family-run Italian company is best known for furs. And who better to make the leap to furrier designer than the king of the pack—fashion's own lion king, Karl Lagerfeld?

Only the richest shopping capitals of the world. →

Paul Smith

The British maestro of menswear (designer of women's and children's too) and unofficial leader of the "lad pack," Paul Smith presents "classics with a twist" and has become one of the industry's most successful exports with more than 220 boutiques worldwide, more than 160 in Japan alone. While his decor is considered too staid by some in London, not so for his new London shop comfortably housed in a Victorian mansion in fashionable Notting Hill Gate with vintage discoveries amongst his collections. It's a whole new retailing concept with the bags to match. We still believe the originals were designed to perfection.

London, Paris, New York, Tokyo.

FENDI

FIFTH AVENUE.

Jil Sander

The simple black bag began with a navy coat. The first German designer to show in Milan, Jil Sander is the queen of clean. She gave women strength without shoulder pads and takes simplicity to the point of art. There's no mistaking a Jil Sander Boutique—it's as clean and modern as her bag and clothes. So is her annual report. No diffusion lines here. Sander's advice is to "buy the best, but buy less." Don't clutter the bag.

Simply *everywhere* in Germany. Plus, France, Switzerland, Italy, Canada, U.S., Hong Kong, Japan, South Korea, and Singapore.

Givenchy

Nothing says French fashion as clearly as Givenchy. As the name rolls off your tongue (zjee-von-cheeeee), a stylish image of Parisian sophistication flashes by, which is precisely how this crisp white bag, accented not in obvious black, but with that perfect French accoutrements—navy blue—looks. The bag is as French as the tradition of the ultimate couture house. Hubert de Givenchy designed Audrey Hepburn's perfect little black dress, and one can see her walking down the Champs Elysées in that same dress swinging this bag. Critics fear that the walls of the House of Givenchy are crumbling, now that Britain's Alexander McQueen is at the helm, deconstructing fashion's elegant past by ripping into it. McQueen is as outrageous as Givenchy is French. "C'est la vie," murmur the French, who have taken McQueen into their hearts and wallets. But our favorite comment was in the *Financial Times:* "McQueen garnered bags of lovely publicity." Let's hope his revolution stops short of the bag.

Paris, New York, Tokyo, with franchises in Moscow and Rome.

According to Jil Sander, her
design style is
"a process of continual correction."
ll, 1998

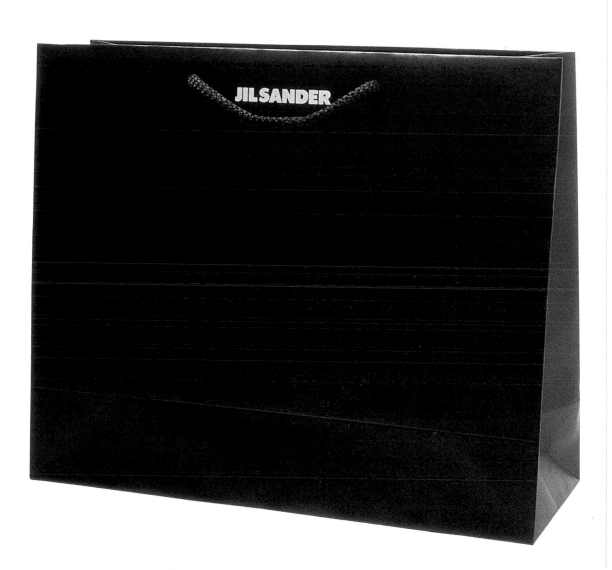

Dolce & Gabbana

Italy's passion-fashion duo. One from the South, the other from the North, their first collection exploded on the scene in 1985 and hasn't stopped since. The yin and yang of Domenico and Stefano is all over the black-and-white bag, as is their pointed sex theme, demonstrated by the razor-sharp white A's in the logo. By bringing the corset out of the closet straight into their bags, they sexified fashion. The subtler black-on-black D&G diffusion-line bag masks the in-your-face D&G logoed clothes. Not that this passion-fashion duo can ever be diffused.

Wherever the passion-fashion flock. →

Nicole Farhi

Born in Nice, trained in Paris, Nicole Farhi first brought her design savvy to London in the early '70s when she and then husband Stephen Marks set up French Connection. The connection worked well. By 1983 she had her own collection and it didn't take long before she became one of the most popular designer labels in British women's closets and one of the highest sales-per-square-foot figures at London's shopping mecca Harvey Nichols. The New York Connection is next, when Farhi brings her collections to her latest flagship store. Although she's redesigning her logo, let's hope she brings the bag as is, with its wonderful, sturdy, dependably chic and understated leather handles.

Eight stores in London, one each in Manchester, Oslo, and Tokyo.

D&G's 1998 spring collection was considered blasphemous. Maybe that's why Madonna loves their clothes.

DOLCE & GABBANA

"I keep trying to turn the volume down, not up.
It's clarification we need, not abundance."
Donna Karan, *Vogue*, 1998

Their campaign is:
DKNY: the official
uniform of New York.

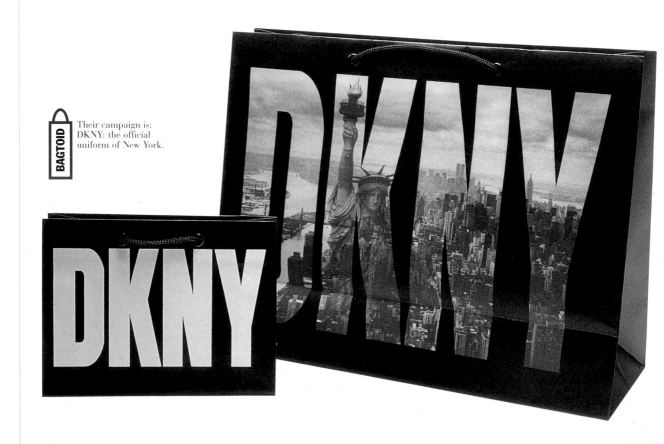

"I love the way the Joseph carrier bag is so simple, clean and graphic. It is a design that makes a mark in everyone's mind even if it is not a conscious observation. to last in people's memories for years to come. It is a classic!"
Joseph

We applaud the design and the designer who still stops in his shop every few days to read the autograph book and learn what his customers think.

Joseph

Moroccan-born, British fashion leader Joseph Ettedgui opened his first clothing store inside his hair salon in London in the '70s. Now in many boutiques you can buy almost anything that fashion dictates, but you can't get a haircut. Just as he sells the pants anyone can look good in, Joseph has *the* carrier bag every-one's got to have. When he briefed graphic designer Teresa Raviras about the concept for the carrier bag to replace the black-and-white pho-tograph by Pamela Hanson, he said he wanted something just as strik-ing. "Chic, contemporary, but also timeless." Raviras came up with the uneven stripes in black against stark white, with slight variations for the men's and women's bags. The design is both very sleek, Audrey Hepburn of the '50s and '60s, and very city chic.

London, New York, Paris, Germany, Cannes.

DKNY

Donna Karan is as New York as you can get—just look at the bag. Trained at Parsons, she understands real women and their bodies. She understands the power of black.

Wherever real women are.

Kenzo

If you go to a French wedding, 60 percent of the women will be dressed in Kenzo. From bold-colored flowers to jungle prints, the designs reflect Kenzo's great sense of color and fun. So are his bags, designed in a color palette all his own. While his ad copy reads, "Creations for a more beautiful world," his bags get the same message across with a simple subtlety. Among the legions of his fans is Naomi Campbell's mother (who might be mistaken for her twin sister—talk about good genes). She wears Kenzo and tells Fashion File TV that "it's comfortable to wear. I'm wearing one now. Simple, but elegant. None of the razzmatazz."

Where the world is beautiful.

Sonia Rykiel

The golden logo on her classy black bag reflects the golden red hues of her very French coiffeur. And the textured lines are as neat and smooth as her classic jersey and knitwear. She was the pioneer designer on Paris's Left Bank when she opened her boutique in 1968 (at the same time the students were having a different kind of revolution) and made clothes that liberated women. Now the "Queen of Knits" owns the street, with separate women's, men's, and children's boutiques, and has plenty of other designer company.

Where liberated people shop.

"The Rykiel woman? She always has a bag on her shoulders
so that she can stride forward—with a child in each hand."
Sonia Rykiel, *International Herald Tribune*, 1998

Louis Vuitton

Just when you thought the LV status logo couldn't become more popular, American Marc Jacobs has joined the company that started as a master trunk-maker in 1854. LV is above all a legend, bridging the art of travel with the art of good living. The bag is a work of art too, with three-quarters of it in grained paper, color toned (cipango gold) to look (and feel) just like the epi-leather bag line. The last quarter turns smooth to the top with toledo blue cord handles.

The LV initials are found wherever it's chic to be.

Céline

The most low-key member of the LVMH empire. Although rumored to be taking on yet another British-crazed fashion lad (Antonio Berardi), they opted to go across the Atlantic and hire the American Michael Kors, a move calculated to hold on to the ladies who sit at the head of the table, either at lunch or in the boardroom. This classic, elegant bag fulfills Céline's promise that the "Céline client will always appear chic and at ease," particularly when carrying the bag.

More than 100 worldwide—all with the same design specifications so that the client will always feel comfortably at home.

"The LV monogram is such an icon I wanted to make it both **visible and invisible in a sleek, young contemporary way.**"

Marc Jacobs, creative director, *W*, 1998

Did the $500 limited edition 1998 LV World Cup football get wrapped in a bag? Let's hope the customers were permitted to carry it in their hands.

[Margiela] "is using the shape and function of the shopping bag— when you open the shopping bag and have a hole in it. then you have a garment."

New Yorker, 1998

BAGTOID Jean-Louis Dumas Hermés (fifth generation Hermés) has courageously hired one of the most controversial designers around—Martin Margiela—for Women Ready to Wear. We applaud the choice, in part, because of his plastic shopping bag T-shirts.

HERMÈS
24, FAUBOURG SAINT-HONORÉ, PARIS

Hermès

One look at this bag and it's no surprise that Thierry Hermès began as a saddle maker way back in 1837. What is a surprise is how the bags came to be the color and texture they are. Before WWII, the bags were decorated with a pale beige paper, reminiscent of pigskin. But during the Occupation, the reserves diminished and it was impossible to obtain coupons for something as frivolous as packaging, so Hermès made do with a solid orange colored cardboard that the supplier had. After the war, orange was selected once again as a reminder of those times. This time it was grainier and livelier and became as identifiable with Hermès as the logo, the scarves, ties, and the Kelly bag.

One hundred sixty-nine stores worldwide.

Loewe

Pronounced Low-ay-vay, a name so soft, it almost sounds like leather. This Spanish luxury leathergoods house, founded in 1846, has always been known for its discreet image. In fact, the Spanish royal family are among their patrons. No surprise that the design and the logo on the bag have a majestic Spanish feel. The royal connection continues with Narciso Rodriguez joining Loewe as the new design director. He shot to fame at Cerruti when he designed for America's royal family—the Kennedys—by creating the ivory crepe wedding dress for Carolyn Bessette Kennedy.

Madrid, London, and New York.

Valentino's signature "V"
touch is marked in the seams
of his couture clothing . . .
as it is on his bag.

In 1963, Yves Saint Laurent was **the first living designer to be honored by the Metropolitan Museum of Art.** We hope the bag was included in the exhibit.

No one can speak better for YSL than the man himself: "I am happy to be copied." Yves Saint Laurent, *W*, 1998 "He's my hero." Marc Jacobs, *W*, 1998 "He's done things that are divine." Karl Lagerfeld *W*, 1998

Valentino

Valentino restores faith in high fashion. Just look at his bags—with exquisite simplicity and geometric shapes in couture colors, there's a bag for every generation. Among the jewels in his crown is one of Jackie Kennedy's wedding dresses and countless ballgowns for La Liz (Taylor). While he was still designing, he sold his company to HdP (which owns Fiat) for 300 million dollars. Pass this bag down to the next generation for safekeeping.

Where the highly fashionable shop.

Yves Saint Laurent

Yves Saint Laurent is bigger than his bag. A fashion phenomenon at 21 at the House of Dior, by 25 he was on his own with fashion's first meaningful initials YSL. He defined what it meant to be chic: Catherine Deneuve's black dress in *Belle de Jour*, the smoking tuxedo suit and his colorful Mondrian-like dresses, which inspired the Rive Gauche shopping bag. Today everyone copies him—even Yves Saint Laurent himself. He'll still be copied until at least year 2016 (when his current contract ends).

Where the highly fashionable designers window shop.

The first designer boutique on Madison Avenue—replaced a supermarket!

BAGLOID

In 1998, Yves Saint Laurent handed over the reigns of his Rive Gauche collection to Alber Elbaz, but don't panic: Yves Saint Laurent is still devoted to haute couture.

Anya Hindmarch

If a bag designer can't design a collectible shopping bag, who can? Anya doesn't disappoint. When she was 18, Anya went to Florence and returned to London with a drawstring and a concept. She was commissioned by *Harpers & Queen* to design a special promotion bag; five hundred were sold which financed her own business. A decade later she's designing handbags and accessories for the fashion pack. Her carrier bag is a shopper-stopper. She has created a distinct striped bag with an extra hole for ribbon closure at the top. No one will be able to get into the bag to steal it.

Two stores in London, one in Hong Kong.

Christian Lacroix

"It's Lacroix, dahling," oozed Ab Fab's Eddy to explain all fashion misdemeanors. Lacroix may have been indirectly responsible for the overindulgent opulent '80s, but you've got to love him. After studying fashion in Paris and designing at Jean Patou, Bernard Arnault (of LVMH) financed Lacroix's own house, making him the only French designer in the LVMH stable. In the world of black and beige, Lacroix screams life and color. Just look at these bags—they're as original as he is. So is Bazaar, one of the best diffusion lines in the business, with one of the all-time best bags.

Russia, Switzerland, Japan, Taiwan, U.S., and of course, Paris.

When asked what have been his greatest moments in fashion,
Christian Lacroix replied,

"The cheers of my friends
from the South at my first show,
just like at a bullfight. . . .

Tears in the eyes of my clients at the end of a show."
Fashion 2000

Guess what Hervé Leger's
favorite color is?

Hervé Leger

Enter the store and you are in a lavender salon, complete with cloud-like walls, satin-cushioned seats, with bags to match. Hervé Leger has taken it as far as it can go. Banding (old couture)/bondaging (new couture) is Leger's specialty. He uses bands of stretch lycra to create the body of Venus on any woman who can not only afford it, but also wear it. Is it fair that these women also get this exquisite lavender fantasy bag?

Paris only, naturellement!

Pink

Despite its name and color, this is not a women's lingerie store. Named for Thomas Pink, London's best tailor in the late 18th century, whose works of quality inspired the phrase "in the pink," this store boasts one of the largest collections of shirts, ties and cufflinks primarily for men. Oddly enough, Thomas Pink was famous for his handmade hunting jackets (called Pink Coat or hunting pink) and by all accounts never made a shirt. The change from the traditional white plastic bag with the red fox was made 18 months ago to appeal to a wider, international clientele, according to its owner and designer, James Mullen. While the color pink was risky, finishing it off with a masculine black border worked. More than 500,000 bags hit the streets in a year in England, Ireland, and the U.S.

London, Dublin, Edinburgh, Glasgow, New York. →

Mullen's favorite bags? "Tiffany's and Hermès."

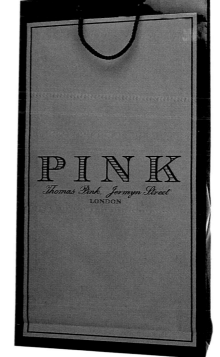

PINK

Thomas Pink, Jermyn Street
LONDON

"She blasted an opening in the wall of tradition. . . ."
London Museum Catalogue

Martine Sitbon

Edgy and sharp are the words most often used to describe Martine Sitbon's creations . . . and one look at these bags lets you know she's not your mother's fashion designer. Her stuff rocks. So if you see a whole lot of shaking going on in these plastic bags, don't be surprised.

One store in Paris. →

Mary Quant

Her signature was a daisy. Her place—King's Road, then the world. Her invention—the miniskirt. Her time—the '60s. When London was the center of the universe, Mary Quant dressed and colored all the major players. Forty years later, she colors on, with a makeup collection of more colors than years she's been in business, as well as crop tops and, yes, miniskirts, among other clothing. The daisy is still stuck on everything, including the shopping bag, giving '60s power to a '90s girl.

London.

"I am living my own obsession and my obsession is women.
I try to make women happy."
Emanuel Ungaro, CNN, *Style*, 1998

His shopping bags do.

Emanuel Ungaro

The Ungaro woman is a woman who dresses for men. Day or evening, the clothes are as far from unisex and the boardroom as you can go. Sensual fabrics, luscious colors, exquisite florals, the clothes drape the body emphasizing the female form. Then why have the bags changed from the unique rose/red to black or white? What happened to the beautiful flowered bag? We can only believe that the sale to Ferragamo had something to do with this. The bag is far more conservative than its contents. Bring back the flash.

Paris, Bal Harbour, Guam, Geneva, Hong Kong, Milan, New York, Palm Beach, Prague, Rome, Seoul, and Tapei.

Patrick Cox

Wannabe. It all began when Cox saw Kiss's Gene Simmons's platform boots. Canadian by birth, he studied his craft in London where Jimmy Choo was a classmate. His big break was almost by mistake. Designing the shoes for a Vivienne Westwood fashion show, his rejected gold platform shoes accidentally walked on stage and captured the imagination of the fashion world. It's history now, as is his wannabe bag. But the Patrick Cox bag lives on—inspired by a fleur-de-lys print on a beautiful blue carpet.

Nine stores including London, New York, and Paris.

"The carpet was from the Louis XIV Palace Fontainebleau. Every season I would visit Paris and look at the carpet, longing to buy it but could never afford it. By the time I had enough money, the carpet was gone— the idea stayed with me and became my signature."
Patrick Cox

Voyage

There's a long line outside and a bouncer. It's in London's fashionable Chelsea and it's not a club. It's not advertised. Members only. But everyone wants to get in. Because any store you can't get into must be great. So it goes with London's latest shopping sensations—Voyage for Women, Voyage for Men. Run by the owners, a husband-and-wife team who were former designers for Valentino and their children, each item is an almost one-off, updated vintage clothing with colors changing weekly. Madonna wears their clothes, so do Emma Thompson and Melanie Griffith. But the real find are the carrier bags. If you can get in, buy anything to get the bags. We prefer the colors of the men's bags—in particular the vibrant purple, turquoise, or gold, but the women's are beautiful too. All adorned with ribbon, tassels, and a clear card that reads "Living in Voyage." If only you can get in.

London only.

Inès de la Fressange

Is there life after being Karl Lagerfeld's muse on the runway? There certainly is, if you are Inès de la Fressange. With a women's clothing shop as bright and cheerful as her pastel, striped, scalloped bags, she's got the whole French nation cheering her on. The clothes are designed for women with real lives and the new range of La Maison d'Inès for real living. No matter what you buy, the bag is worth it. Come on, who'd ever throw this one away?

One store in Paris.

"The idea of the look is not too much. **not to match.**"
according to Voyage store manager, Antoine.

"We're inspired by the people in the street."
Voyage's Tiziano Mazzilli, *OK!* 1998

When Donna Karan presented Yohji Yamamoto with the Fashion Group Award, she said,
"I'm a designer, not an artist.
But this man, this man is an artist."

Thierry Mugler

This ice blue bag spells sex with attitude. No matter what size or shape you are, when you put a Mugler suit on, it's all curve and you are in cool control. Razor-sharp S&M flashes turned into feminine Amazon power plays. With Jerry Hall as his muse, it's no wonder. "You can always wear his clothes. He's timeless." (Jerry Hall, Fashion File TV) But not everyone thinks so. When asked if she would ever wear his clothes, actress Tippy Hedren replied, "In the real world? I don't think so." (Fashion File TV)But whatever you think of his clothes, you can always wear his bag.

Two stores in Paris.

Yohji Yamamoto

Yohji Yamamoto's deep electric blue unstructured felt-like paper bag is just like his clothes. He designs for "a woman who has given up being a woman. But she is incredibly sexy to me." And his bag has almost given up being a bag (it can be worn anywhere on the body). His following is pretty diverse too: Charlotte Rampling, Tina Turner, Carolyn Bessette Kennedy, Robin Williams, Sting, and Karl Lagerfeld.

Tokyo, Paris, New York, London, Antwerp, and Zurich.

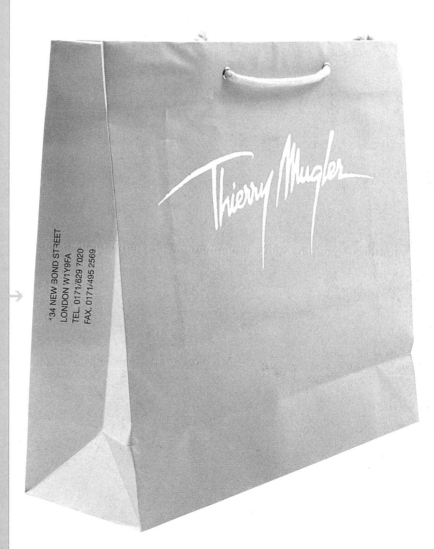

134 NEW BOND STREET
LONDON W1Y9FA
TEL. 0171/629 7020
FAX. 0171/495 2569

Chapter 2
DESIGNER STORES

VINTAGE COLLECTIONS.
FASHION'S ROYALTY. CUTTING-EDGE DESIGN.
THESE STORES GIVE NEW MEANING
TO THE FASHION TERM MIX AND MATCH.
WHEN YOU'RE OUT LOOKING.
BUT NOT SURE WHAT YOU'RE LOOKING FOR.
THESE BAGS LEAD YOU RIGHT INTO THE MOST EXCITING DESIGNER STORES.

Yellow Rat Bastard

This bag screams hip-hop-cool! It's the bright yellow of a stop sign and you can't miss those bold black letters. But unlike a stop sign, the other side has its very own design. Check it out. It's as downtown New York as you can get. Wide pants, narrow pants, striped pants. This store has stuff and more stuff. The staff is as laid back as the stuff. In fact, it's not a bad place to hang; you'll probably even find something to buy. And it would be worth it—for the Yellow Rat Bastard bag.

There's only one Yellow Rat Bastard—in Soho, New York.

Felissimo

In the midst of New York's midtown frenzy there's one store that offers a respite. Felissimo is a one-of-a-kind store selling one-of-a-kind items. It's a store with a total Eastern philosophy that touches everything, even its packaging, which was designed not to shout but to whisper its name *felissimo*. In order to bring nature to this urban retreat, each shopping bag has a natural closure made from a birch twig taken only from trees already felled. If ever the merchandise within a store was so crafted to fit the bag that carries it—this is the place. Nothing is out of whack—it all fits together like natural pieces of a whole-earth puzzle. If you need to cool out before you shop, head straight to the Haiku Cafe, guaranteed to calm you down and lift your spirits—almost as much as lifting one of these bags will.

One store only in New York.

STEINBERG
& TOLKIEN

193 Kings Road,
Chelsea London SW3 5EB
Telephone: 071-376 3660

*Antique Designer Costume,
Jewellery, Vintage &
Contemporary Clothing
& Accessories*

Steinberg & Tolkien

There are few fashion designers who haven't been here, or haven't at least sent their assistants. Walk in and you think you're in one of London's many thrift shops. Look around and you realize this is one of the world's best stores—a selling museum with clothes coded on racks by the decade, hats, jewelry, vintage shoes. The owner is a hoarder, and sometimes his finds precipitate what will be on the catwalk the following season. Inquire about an item, and there's probably a story attached to it. The only disappointment is the plastic carrier bag—not vintage enough for our tastes.

Only one Steinberg & Tolkien (grandson of author JRR and son-in-law of Steinberg) on London's famous King's Road

Maria Luisa

Venezuelan–born Parisian Maria Luisa knows how to select her designers. One trip to this shop and you can be outfitted for a season in a collage of all the latest without even thinking. Shalom stops by, as does Nicole Kidman, Tom Cruise and Juliette Binoche. The shiny black bag hides the source so everyone will think you spent days shopping.

Paris only, on the fashionable rue de Cambon.

"How do I love thee? Let me count the shopping bags. . . ."

"I have often been tempted to update our carrier. but it is so synonymous with Browns and, of course, our customers love it!" Joan Burstein

The Library

The ideal place to shop is surrounded by books. You can't help but feel smart in this environment. As you will with the bag, designed to look like the rich inside cover of an antique leather-bound book. It is also a smart place to shop for men's clothing, owned by the former manager of Joseph's menswear division; the fashion is knowledgeably selected.

Only one, now in London's fashionable Chelsea.

Browns/Browns Focus

If there's only time for one store in London, then Browns is the place to go for a sampling of the best of the design world, established and new. Owner Joan Burstein has developed a reputation for taking the hottest labels from the catwalk and discovering new talent (she was one of John Galliano's early supporters). It must run in the family, for when her daughter (Caroline Collis) opened Browns Focus, which concentrates on introducing young designers names and attracting future Browns customers, the *London Fashion Guide* declared, "She (Caroline Collis) has seen the future and it has a label on it!"

Stores in London only.

According to *W*, the best place to spot celebrities in Hollywood
is at Fred Segal's.
"The preferred look, unlike the merchandise,
is grungy and incognito."
The only thing it can't hide is the bag.

Koh Samui

There's nothing about this store that isn't cool. It's on London's cool Monmouth Street, it features the brightest and best of Britain's young design set (clothes, jewelry, shoes, accessories), and sends them on their way. If you buy it here, you've seen it first and deserve to be seen with the bag.

Only one store in London.

Ron Herman/
Fred Segal Melrose

In the Land of Fashion Angels—and those with a devilish twinkle—there's only one place to check out all the latest fashions: Fred Segal's. Comprised of small boutiques, such as Ron Herman's, there's a boutique for every style as long as it's hip, young, expensive, and exclusive. This is one store that needs no advertising because this is where all of new Hollywood shops. The clothes speak for themselves, as does any bag carrying this logo.

Ron Herman: two stores in LA—Brentwood and Melrose;
Fred Segal: two stores in LA—Melrose and Santa Monica.

koh samui

65 Monmouth Street, Covent Garden, WC2. TEL: 0171-240 4280

Now that the individual look is "in,"
stores that sell an interesting mix of the latest collections
and provide necessary friendly advice are also in.
Here are two of London's top draws:

Tokïo/The Cross

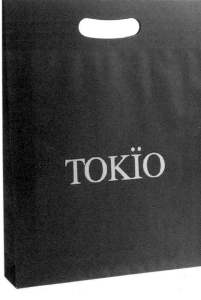

Tokïo

Situated at Brompton Cross, Tokïo is a boutique devoted to discovering new designers and keeping them. The clothes are not displayed by designer, so the customer will feel freer to put things together creatively. It must work because among the clientele are Madonna(does she shop all the time?), Nicole Kidman, Goldie Hawn, and Kate Moss. Maybe they come for the bag too—it's raspberry pink and fun and "designed to give the customer an up-lifting feeling when they leave the shop."

London.

The Cross

Sam and Sarah went to school together, shopped together, and now own The Cross together. Their buying philosophy—anything they'd like for themselves—keeps this low-key store eclectic and fun with merchandise for the home, the self and the child. Its Notting Hill location provides a shopping sanctuary, and its discreet bag a good way of disguising those expensive purchases from prying eyes.

London.

Chapter 3
MASS APPEAL

THEY'RE ON THE STREETS.
THEY'RE ON BILLBOARDS.
THEY'RE ON TV.
THEY ARE THE BRAND NAMES WE CAN'T LIVE WITHOUT.
CARRY THESE BAGS AND YOU'LL FIT IN EVERYWHERE.
IT'S THE WORLD OF MASS APPEAL.

BAGTOID

This is one shopping bag that says much more than the clothes that fill it. It lives beyond its name and gives new and true meaning to the term "United Colors of Benetton."

United Colors of Benetton

This store invented the formula that has changed the lives of millions of people all over the world by displaying all its merchandise on shelves folded and color-coordinated. It gave a military look which fit in nicely with the legions of Benetton Army fans who clamored to buy these clothes. There was a time in the '80s when there seemed to be a Benetton on every other block. The hype has died down, but the style lives on. Who could have imagined they would take over the landmark Scribner Building and replace the books with sweaters?

Franchises worldwide

McDonald's

There's no question about what's in this bag. You can smell the fries a mile away. It's a family bag. It's a carrier bag. It's a fast-food bag. You eat what's in it, and you throw it away. It's a good thing it's recyclable, because it's the world's most popular bag.

Anywhere you might be—we've heard that a new one opens every three hours some place in the world.

"SONY . . . so New York."
Jerry Seinfeld, *Vanity Fair*

Gap

Gap's shopping bag is not just a container emblazoned with the company logo. A solid blue square, printed with Gap in white, the bag actually becomes the logo in three-dimensional form.. And this is not by chance. Gap's clean, modern image is carefully crafted and maintained. From the store's straightforward window displays to the trademark white space in both print and TV advertising, to the democratic style of the clothing Gap sells, everything about the brand is as smart, confident, and consistent as the bag itself.

More locations than one can count.

Sony Style

You can buy almost anything you might want—TVs, CDs, videos, stereos, books, calendars, mugs, and so much more—in the store that merges electronics with TV, film, music, and licensing deals. (You can even buy Starbucks coffee.)

"SONY . . . so New York," deadpanned Jerry Seinfeld to *Vanity Fair*. But was he referring to this Japanese megaconglomorate that has conquered the world of entertaining, or the Sony Style shopping bags with the New York skyline so artfully displayed on both sides?

More locations than any equipment junkie dreamed possible.

Urban Outfitters

This now-legendary chain store was hip the day it was born in 1976—as the bag clearly states—and it's even more popular today with its second-generation customers clamoring to get inside. It has come full circle—just like the bag.

Wherever urbanites need to be outfitted. →

Tommy Hilfiger

Tommy Hilfiger's career began in menswear, but now everyone wants his clothes, including rap stars everywhere. The youth of America—the X, Y, and Z generations salute Tommy's flag which they wear proudly on most of the clothing and which flows freely on the shopping bag in their hands. Tommy aficionados come in all shapes and sizes from all strata of life. The $500,000 Tommy Tour Bus, overflowing with the offspring of the rich and famous, journeyed from New York to Los Angeles, with stops at stores along the way, to promote his newest line of Tommy Jeans. Crowds came out to cheer the bus on—waving their Tommy shopping bags.

New York, London, and Paris. →

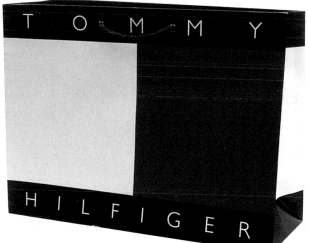

Canal Jean Company

There's only one Canal Jean in downtown New York City, but everyone seems to know it—even the European and Japanese tourists who flock to the store and go home with suitcases stuffed with jeans. With a bag as identifiable as the store—plastic, practical, and the first to be slung over the shoulder—it's a bag that can be worn anytime, anywhere, over and over. This is the store that invented New York streetwear, and the uniform never varies from generation to generation—jeans, jeans, jeans. The store has "endless rows of Levis, Calvins, socks, and undies. Plus, an entire floor of vintage 501 clothing" *The Guardian* (UK, 1997). We describe it as street heaven in a bag.

Only one, in New York City.

Tower Records

The legend began in Los Angeles on Sunset Boulevard where Tower Records was the cool place to buy records. The rest is history. This yellow bag is by far the most recognizable in the music industry and is multitalented: it doubles as a receptacle in cars for flotsam, leak-proof lunch bag, distinctive rain hat, etc. Other uses are still being developed for the large bag with its red trip fastener running the length of the top of the bag.

New York, Los Angeles, London, and Paris.

Rolling Stones's
Keith Richards
must have lots of
Tower shopping bags
in his apartment because
he used to live above
the New York's East Village store.
We wonder whose records he bought?

TOWER®

"In 1988 our goal was to create our shopping bag as moving billboards.
Since GUESS? stores are unisex, we selected an image
showing a young couple.
The logo is carefully positioned to enhance brand identity
without conflicting with the image."
Art Direction, Paul Marciano; Packaging Design, Kumiko Morishita

GUESS?

There's no guessing about what's in this bag. Everyone knows these are the sexiest jeans around. And it's no surprise that three French brothers designed them and then discovered Bridget Bardot look-alike Claudia Schiffer to market their wares. From a pair of GUESS? jeans begat the GUESS? empire: GUESS? for babies, kids, boys, girls, teens, and adults. Because we may grow up, but guess what? We'll never outgrow our love of Guessing.

Guess? Everywhere!

Kenneth Cole

Not everyone takes a political stand—even when standing in sturdy, supportive shoes. But Kenneth Cole is never one to stand back. Almost as lauded as his shoes and bags are his advertising slogans, which appeal to the masses. Here's an example: "We the people . . . know it's a woman's right to choose. After all, she's the one carrying it." And what most Kenneth Cole fans are carrying is this shopping bag. Proudly chosen because it's strong and fresh, with a sense of humor belying a powerful message layered beneath a great pair of shoes. It's a heavy load to lay in any paper bag—but this one can handle it.

Found wherever people need to make a stand—
standing comfortably.

Chapter 4
SEX APPEAL

A WHIFF OF ROMANCE,
A SNAP OF THE GARTER.
A HIGH ON STILETTOES,
A RUSH FROM CHOCOLATE.
THESE ARE THE BAGS THAT FUEL THE FANTASIES
AND ARE FILLED WITH SEX APPEAL.

Diptyque

The French have long understood the secret of the scent, and the Diptyque candle is a Parisian classic. With more than 36 scents, there's one for everyone, and pleasant hours can be whiffed away making the right choice and identifying the logo on each glass. But the logo on the bag is universally recognized and what's in the bag will be no secret when you leave the store.

Only one diptyque, one Paris, one Boulevard St. Germain.

Jimmy Choo

The Choo shoe steps out and makes a statement with its slim, tall heel and T-strap and can be seen adorning only the best-kept feet at every fashionable event on the social calendar. Until recently the Malaysian-born master's shoes were only available for the select few and custom made. Now the upper masses can stop by his boutique to see if the slender shoe fits. If not, there are lovely handbags which will fit perfectly into the deep wine-colored glossy carrier bag with the silver logo which makes a statement all of its own.

London—on the same street as Christian Louboutin.

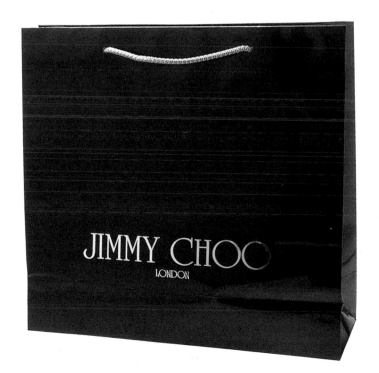

"I feel I'm doing something right if people smile."
Westwood told Video Fashion on E TV in 1998.
Who wouldn't smile with one of her bags?

Vivienne Westwood

Sex sells . . . and no one knows that better than Vivienne Westwood, who named one of her first stores after one of her favorite things—SEX. From the mother of punk (the legendary band The Sex Pistols met in her store) to the grande dame of British fashion, Vivienne Westwood defies definition. She was the first British designer to show in Paris since Mary Quant, was named by John Fairchild as one of the six most influential designers of all time, and was awarded an OBE by the Queen in 1992, but she still never abandoned her punk roots. Her shop, The End of the World, has a clock forever winding backwards, but she's as forward thinking as any of the younger British designer lads. With diverse fashion lines running the gamut from made-to-measure haute couture to MAN, her men's line, she's got a bag for every line, which are as distinct as the lines and as beautiful.

London.

Agent Provocateur

Not only is Westwood the mother of punk, she's also the mother of Joseph Corre, co-owner of one of the best-named lingerie stores in the world: Agent Provocateur. Designed in boudoir style, there's something for every taste in this London Soho store, including the bags—in pink or black with lavender print. In fact, London's most popular lingerie shop has become a tourist destination and *the* place to obtain the complete bedroom look from garments to those necessary bedtime accessories and jewels.

Only one in London's Soho. →

"The point of appeal for the shop is that anybody may find something to suit their fetishes or fancies." Joseph Corre

"Beautiful Marquise,
your creations tempt me
to damnation."
French actor Bruno Kremer's comments in the visitor's book.

BAGTOID

If you don't want to cover
up your toes with a bag,
then make time for the
on-site pedicure.

La Marquise de Sévigné

La Marquise de Sévigné ("Say-veen-yay") has been a temptress for more than 100 years, realizing that Christopher Columbus's most important discovery wasn't necessarily America, but the cocoa bean from which chocolate is made. In 1935, Pope Puis XI, who knew the Paris store, is alleged to have told the owner's wife, "If all roads lead to Rome, they could also take you from Rome to Boulevard de la Madeleine," where the store was located. Other celebrities and mere mortals have come back again and again to this den of iniquity, unable to avoid its magnetic appeal. And famous artists have created designs for the boxes to house their sweets (Raoul Dufy, Salvador Dali, Jean-Charles de Castelbajac). The deep blue mosaic bag is as rich as its contents, but ever so much more seductive full than empty.

Three stores in Paris, eleven others in France, one in Beirut, Alexandria, Buenos Aires, Saigon, Madrid, Stockholm, Mexico, Montevideo, and Beijing.

Gina

Conveniently located right beside all those other trendy Sloane Street shops, Gina has been around for a century. With a reputation for meticulous craftsmanship as good as its longevity—up to twenty stitches per inch—these shoes are aimed for the fashionably clad and are flaunted on the catwalks and all the fashion magazines. Still we find the bags, with their silver and gold shoes, the best show of all and almost as meticulously produced!

Only one Gina on London's Sloane Street, but two brothers run the store.

Christian Louboutin

One look in Christian Louboutin's store and you know this is a designer who enjoys what he does. Each shoe is displayed on its own inset shelf, and the boutique looks more like a salon than a store. You don't just sit to try on shoes, you recline. Or you get them designed to order just like Princess Caroline of Monaco, Cher, Naomi Campbell, and Elle Macpherson do. While his shoes are some of the most beautiful around, if you are in the market for innovation, he provides that too—from heels made of Guinness cans to giant silk daisy buckles.

Paris and London.

Charbonnel et Walker

It all started in 1875 when Edward VII (then Prince of Wales), who had a taste for the frequent sweet, convinced Mme Charbonnel to leave the chocolate house of Maison Bossier in Paris to join Mrs. Walker in London and start a confectionery house on Bond Street. Noel Coward had boxes sent around the world to him wherever he was; John Gielgud and his Aunt Ellen Terry both had their own selections. And, after all these years, they are still a royal favorite, note the Royal Warrant (rose violet creams are the Queen Mum's fave). As good as the chocolate is, so is the packaging and the promise carried by the bag.

London, the Royal Arcade.

"I'm not into comfort, but my shoes do have to serve as something between a weapon and an objet d'art."
Christian Louboutin

"When choosing between
two shopping bags,
I always try the one I've never tried before."

Mae West

Janet Reger

While Mary Quant was raising the hems of the skirt, Janet Reger was making sure that what might be seen would be worth looking at. She put color and fun in matched-set underwear and set the trend that's been followed ever since. With celebrities like Bianca Jagger and Princess Anne as early clients, her fame spread quickly, her lingerie became a symbol of luxury, and her logo (pink dragonfly) a symbol for sex.

London and Dubai.

D. Porthault

You must sleep better on D. Porthault linen, just knowing that your head is resting on the fabric made by this nearly 80-year-old, 100 percent family-run business. Otherwise, why would Jackie Kennedy, the Duke and Duchess of Windsor, Pamela Harriman, and so many heads of state commission their household linen from them? With over 5,600 patterns and 40 new prints added each year, employing some of the last French craftsmen capable of hand-knotting lace and open-embroidery work, this company has earned the title "grand couturier" of household linen. Its bag is in keeping with the sense of history and tradition featuring the logo created in 1920 by Madeleine Porthault in her "lucky" blue, representing a threaded needle, thimble, and a crown made of dressmaking scissors.

Paris and New York.

Victoria's Secret

Victoria has taken the secret out of sex and showed the world that selling sex isn't sleazy. Known as one of the sexiest stores in the world, it packages lingerie in the most attractive way. The stores look just like the shopping bags, pink and feminine. The only reason not to order through the catalogue is you'll get the goods without the flirty bag.

More than 800 stores in the U.S.

Sabbia Rosa

When your saleswomen wear stilettoes and slips, it's not hard to believe that half of the clients at this store are men. In fact, that seems shockingly low. Madame Rosa has been around for a couple of decades, partially dressing some of the world's most elegant women in luscious silk, handmade lingerie. Madame Rosa understands the age-old secret—sex never stops selling, no matter how high the price, and people always come back for more. It is with this same savvy that her bag is designed. No see-through bag for Madame Rosa. Sturdy yet sophisticated, the bag shows the class of the carrier. The only hint at what's inside is the green scripted name on the bag.

There's only one Sabbia Rosa, and it's in Paris, of course.

Supermodel Karen Mulder (E TV 1998) summed up Victoria's Secret: "It's all about women who feel good about themselves."

NICOLA DE MARIA

Fogal

This Swiss company has put the accent back on the leg. One of the first stores devoted solely to legwear, Fogal put the sex back in the stocking and the garter back on the leg with more patterns and designs and colors than seen before in one place. Equally striking is the carrier bag designed by different artists, with new ones commissioned at least once a year. And we thought the Swiss specialized in chocolate, gold, and neutrality.

In more than 35 countries including the U.S.

Bjorn Borg

This is a most unlikely match—Bjorn Borg and underwear. Yet it's a smash hit. With boutiques throughout Europe and Asia and a steamy catalogue, his underwear wins point after point with the crowd, leading us to believe that there are no unforced errors here. One look at the bag and everyone will know what the game is.

Europe and Asia.

Red or Dead

From its Bohemian beginnings in a stall market in London's Camden Town, Red or Dead has earned the British Street Designer of the Year Award several years running. With stores now on fashionable Sloane Street, Earlham Street, and in Thomas Neal's Centre, they have merchandise that's some of the tackiest, wackiest around. Combine western wear with wallpaper-print loafers, and your ensemble could only have been Red or Dead. Could it be that their too-short trousers have led the capri pants revival?

Very much alive in London, Tokyo, and Prague.

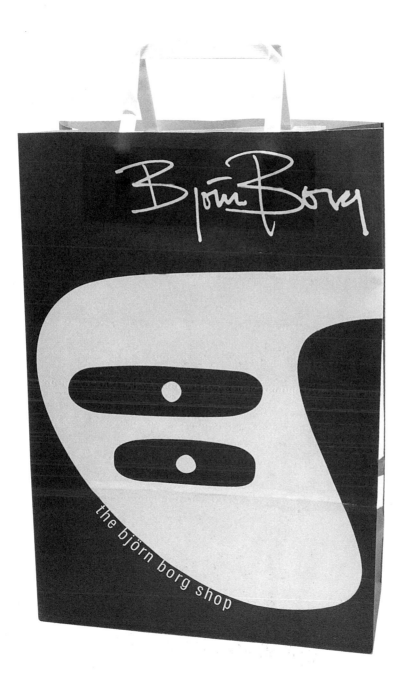

Chapter 5
THE OLD FAITHFULS

THESE BAGS SPEAK A GLOBAL LANGUAGE
THAT NEEDS NO TRANSLATION.
THESE STORES ARE INSTITUTIONS WITH BAGS AS THEIR ICONS
AND PERSONALITIES ALL THEIR OWN
EVERYONE HOLDS ON TO THESE BAGS
BECAUSE THEY CAN BE USED AND REUSED EVEN FOR RETURNS.
JOIN US IN A SALUTE TO: THE OLD FAITHFULS.

"It's cleaner without the apostrophe." Ivan Chermayeff

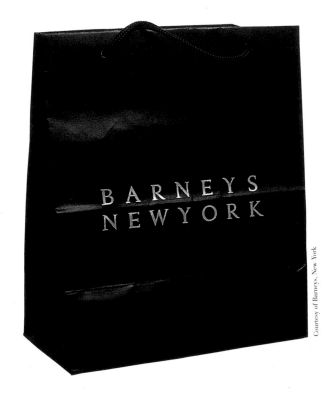

Courtesy of Barneys, New York

Barneys

It's simple, it's black, it's expensive. Just as the merchandise is cutting edge, so is the bag. The quality of the paper is so high that it's colored black during the manufacturing process, and the logo is stamped in silver. It's so subtle that only those under 30 can read the logo on the bag. Yet people of all ages are carrying this bag—and it looks good anywhere.

Seven stores in the U.S.

Century 21

No wonder this is one of the most recognizable and versatile bags on the streets of New York, despite its byline "New York's best secret." Century 21 did it right. They went to their customers and asked them for their bag preference. Their clientele voted for durable and waterproof. Not to mention what goes in it—designer goods on sale for one-tenth of the original price, sometimes even less.

Downtown Manhattan and Bayridge, Brooklyn. →

"Hell on earth, but heaven in fashionland . . . still where else can you get Prada and Gucci goodies for $80?" *New York Observer*

"Paris, France, and the world are our market."
George Meyer, Chairman

Galeries Lafayette

France's most famous department store started in 1894 as Aux Galerie Lafayette, selling novelties such as ribbons and sheer apparel. By 1905, a sign above the door proclaimed "Galeries Lafayette, the best bargain store in all of Paris." But the flagship store, catering to the high-end market, was born in 1912 when it moved to a location in Paris where from the rooftop terrace there was an unobstructed view of the newly erected Eiffel Tower, the perfect symbol for this Parisian landmark store. Today 80,000 visitors a day walk through the door, making the store's objective to "become the retailing choice for every fashion, every impulse, every lifestyle," a reality.

Thrity-four department stores, twenty-nine smaller stores called Nouvelles Galeries.

Bergdorf Goodman

Walk in and it's service, service, service. In fact, look around and you'll see some saleswomen who probably waited on your mother years ago. Not so for the fashion—it's up-to-date, upscale, and upperpriced. With Bonwit's no longer around the corner, it's comforting to know that Bergdorf Goodman still occupies its original spot, a mere step from the Plaza Hotel, a glance away from Tiffany's, a whisper from Bvlgari's, and attached to Van Cleef & Arpels on Fifth Avenue's exclusive upper fifties. And if that's not reassuring enough, do the full tour of the store's boutiques taking in every designer worth knowing, revel in good living on the home accessories floor, and head up to what used to be the exclusive family penthouse apartment, now *the* place to be made over. When you leave, don't forget to take a touch of class with you— the classic Bergdorf's art-deco lilac bag. (Same treatment for men across the street— with a tasteful grey bag).

Only one in New York. →

 Walk out with a M&S bag guilt free, knowing you are demonstrating cents (pence) and sensibility.

Marks & Spencer

Forty percent of the British population wears Marks & Sparks underwear. Begin with these basics and it becomes clear that Marks & Sparks is an institution that is as much a part of life in Britain as a "cuppa" tea. With clothing for the entire family, M&S boasts value for the pound (even if you can't pay with credit cards). Here you will find cotton pyjamas (no longer available in the U.S.) for les enfants terribles, and ready-to-eat meals (for those too busy or tired to cook).

Chains throughout Britain and stores in France where the most popular section is the food hall!

BAGTOID Many still consider F&M to be the authority on correct form and in particular, advice is often asked about the making of tea. At one time they even kept a list of all the major cities in the world with a list of teas suited to the water in each particular city.

Fortnum & Mason

It was 1707 when William Fortnum, a footman to the Royal Household of Queen Anne, persuaded Hugh Mason to go into partnership with him and open a grocery store in Piccadilly. From its humble beginnings as a stall in a doorway on the site of its present building, F&M has served a mere twelve reigns of British monarchy, fed armies and expeditions, sent a huge consignment of concentrated beef tea at Queen Victoria's request to Florence Nightingale to treat the sick, and became a household word, with Charles Dickens and Prime Minister Gladstone as two of their greatest fans. If cool Britannia is too cool for you, Fortnum is the place for some old-fashioned British tradition—from the food halls, to the tea room, to the only clock in London to rival Big Ben. Walk in and walk out with the classic Fortnum blue bag.

Only one store, on Piccadilly, London.
But there *is* a catalogue!

Lacoste

Once upon a time, before Ralph's polo pony, there was an itty bitty green alligator that changed the world of men's casual fashion forever. Nestled discreetly on the side of a soft polo shirt was this alligator. No name mentioned, no name needed. Baby boomers grew up longing to wear this casually chic shirt. But during the '70s and '80s the itty bitty green alligator lay dormant. Now he's back—with more than a polo shirt—and he's got stores everywhere and a bag that's snappier than the alligator ever was. Moral of the story: Everything comes to those who wait.

Wherever you see a tiny green alligator. →

Shanghai Tang

When David Tang Wing-Cheung opened his flagship store in Hong Kong in 1994, his dream of interweaving traditional Chinese cultural elements with 20th/21st-century style was fulfilled. But it wasn't until his New York store opened in 1997 that *Money* magazine declared: "New York's Shanghai Tang will do for all things Chinese what Ralph Lauren's clothing and accessories did for Americana." Not only are the stores unique—with an eclectic blend of accessories and clothing, plus Imperial Tailors offering affordable haute couture—but their shopping bag is worth any purchase.

New York, Hong Kong, and Paris. →

One of the first designer tennis ensembles.

"Nostalgia was our starting point." says Tang. "But we definitely are a store for the 21st century."

BAGTOID In January, 1977,
the Bloomingdale's
shopping bag created havoc.
The bag featured a sleek, slim,
gorgeous girl
with her back to the camera,
long auburn hair, a great smile, and
wearing nothing else. Somehow a rumor
reached WWDaily that the model was
Princess Yasmin (daughter of
Rita Hayworth and Ali Kahn).
While the store was sued for
1.1 million dollars, the actual model,
an NYU student, was the ultimate winner.
The bag caper made her famous
with a feature in the
New York Times Magazine
and the bag became an overnight
collector's item.

Bloomingdale's

Like no other store in the world. The Bloomingdale brothers began their retail endeavor with a Ladies' Notion Shop which expanded in 1872 to the East Side Bazaar. By 1929, Bloomingdale's covered an entire city block, and in 1931, the art-deco edifice that still graces New York City's Lexington Avenue was completed. As innovative as they were with merchandise, so were they with the shopping bag. In 1922, long before the modern shopping bag, Bloomingdale's created a special 50th anniversary message to its customers on the face of its small brown paper bags. It was far from great art, but it was the ancestor of today's famous "Brown Bags." Bloomingdale's first shopping bag with a strong twisted handle was created in 1954, with a rose on one side and an umbrella on the other. But it wasn't until 1961, with the inauguration of its storewide import fairs, that it commissioned the first (designed by Joseph Kinigstein) in a series of designer bags, which often omitted the store's name. Bloomingdale's became famous for its "retail theater," special promotions and accompanying bags, which leading artists, photographers, graphic designers, and fashion designers were engaged to create. Perhaps the most famous was the shopping bag jigsaw puzzle, a montage of the store's favorite bags and proof that for Bloomingdale's, "the shopping bag is no longer a means, but an end in itself."

Twenty-two stores throughout the country.

The legendary Big Brown Bag first hit the streets in 1973. Although it was created to answer the request of the linen department for bigger bags to hold bigger pillows (form follows function), it became so popular that the Little Brown Bag followed a year later, and the trilogy was completed in 1992 with the Medium Brown Bag.

BAGTOID

"A favorite resort of Edina and Patsy,
the shopping-made heroines of the British TV series,
'Absolutely Fabulous,'
who would shriek 'Harvey Nicks!'" *Vogue*, 1997

"Grossed more per square foot
than any other store outside of Japan." *Vogue*, 1997

Harvey Nichols

This fashionholic's heaven was begun by Benjamin Harvey as a linen shop in 1813. Bequeathed to his daughter in 1820, under the condition that she enter into partnership with Colonel Nichols, Harvey Nichols was born, and London has never been the same since. With window displays that stop traffic, the store boasts a clientele that does the same, from Joan Collins to Jamie Lee Curtis to the late Princess Di. With more than 200 top designers, everything about this store is fashionable, from the merchandise, to the restaurants and food hall (with its award-winning bag designed by Michael Nash Associates). Leaving the store can be just as much fun, with a commissionaire stationed at the door to hail a taxi for those weary but fashionably clad feet, and those arms filled with trendy Harvey Nicks' white-and-blue plastic carrier bags.

Knightsbridge and Leeds.

Henri Bendel

This unique department store is almost as well known as the brown-and-white striped bag that carries home its charming message. Founded in 1896 as a millinery store, Henri Bendel was one of the first department stores to create individual boutiques within one location. In fact, Leslie Wexner, the marketing genius of the Limited who now owns Bendels, knew how essential the bag was. He moved the 57th Street store, but insisted on keeping the bag.

After expanding to six stores in the U.S., Henri Bendel is now back where it belongs—one store on New York City's Fifth Avenue.

The Fifth Avenue store incorporates the original Rene Lalique windows.

BAGTOID

Above: Earlier version

Above: This new bag's illustrator, Ed Miller, latched onto the iconography of the communal dressing room, creating an affectionate self-parody of Loehmann's behind-the-scenes.

Loehmann's

In 1920, Frieda Loehmann opened her first store in the basement of her Brooklyn home. The shopping world would never be the same again. First a buyer in a department store, Frieda came up with an ingenious idea—why not buy up the store's overstocked inventory and sell it at a fraction of the cost? The legend of Loehmann's was launched! Generations of women followed their mothers' lead to the racks of Loehmann's; shopping fanatics know which days the best merchandise arrives and stake out the store to be first in when the doors open. When Loehmann's took over the original Barneys' space in New York City in 1997, it was the passing of an era for fashionites, and a flag of victory for those whose shopping mantra is, "You'll never guess how much I paid." Besides bargain prices, the store was best known (and feared) for its communal dressing rooms, as told in Erma Bombeck's best-seller, *Everything I Know About Animal Behavior I Learned in Loehmann's Dressing Room.* But real shoppers know where the secrets are hidden—in the back room, proving that this bag isn't big enough to carry all the goodies home.

Sixty-eight stores in twenty-two states in the USA. Communal dressing rooms still exist, but often alongside private ones.

In 1997, Sophia Loren stopped traffic in the store when she autographed copies of her book. We think the brightly colored bags are traffic-stoppers, too.

Selfridges houses 11 cafes, restaurants, and bars. Who has time to shop?

Selfridges

When Selfridges first opened its doors on March 15, 1909, over 90,000 people came to its party. Looking more like a palace than a shop, over the years Selfridges has boasted many firsts: the first to coin the phrase "only __ shopping days to Christmas," the first playroom where children could be left safely, sale of the world's first television set, and display of the first "themed" Christmas windows containing merchandise.

Selfridges has also claimed its place in history by enabling Winston Churchill to place a call to President Roosevelt through a decoder in the store's basement. But as brilliant as is its history, so is its master plan for the future, highlighted by a subtle reworking of the store's logo to be bolder and more flexible, its trademark yellow color to appear as a fresher "living" yellow, and the dropping of the building from their carrier bags to accommodate plans for new stores in Manchester and Glasgow.

Currently, only London's Oxford Street (though it's a pretty big street and store)! →

The department store (depato) is an essential part of daily life in Tokyo.
It is easy to spend an entire day in one store,
where you can find a travel agency, theater, art gallery, pet shop,
playground, gourmet grocery, and several restaurants.
Not to mention all the merchandise
and the delicate, subtle shopping bags.
Another reason to come here is the service.
As you walk through the store,
salespeople will be standing in positions of attention,
at the proper angle of incline.
Here are two of the best stores (and bags):
Takashimaya/Hankyu

Takashimaya

While Takashimaya Japan's shopping bag may be more traditional than Takashimaya New York's, it more than holds its own—filled with some of the most beautiful kimonos in all of Japan. This is where the Imperial family shops. It's also where the younger set goes to find sophisticated designer labels, traditional Japanese tableware, antiques, and everyday tea sets. We'd go just for the bag.

Hankyu

This is the leading department store headquartered in Osaka with branches throughout Japan. Hankyu windows in Kyoto even display food from the store's two restaurant floors with prices of each dish clearly marked. Whether you eat or shop there, don't leave without one of these extraordinary bags.

Ten thousand shoes are part of the collection in the Salvatore Ferragamo Museum in Florence, Italy. They were all designed by the company founder from 1927 to 1960. Ferragamo was known as an architect of footwear and a shoemaker to the stars. Among the highlights: Marilyn Monroe's stilettoes with reinforced, metal heels.

BAGTOID

Salvatore Ferragamo

Famous for shoes of many widths (translation: designer shoes that you can actually walk in), and world-renowned for the dependable shoes with the wide bow in every color, it's no wonder that Ferragamo's customers are among the most faithful. So when you spot a woman carrying a Ferragamo shopping bag, it's a pretty good bet that she's no virgin Ferragamo buyer. For the 1998 film "Ever After," a remake of the Cinderella story, Ferragamo designed the glass slipper. Cost: $5,500. Small price to pay to become a princess. While the Ferragamo bag is always good to have, the one that every collector really wants is the special color-dominated design by Tanaka Ikko for the centennial exhibition of shoes from the Ferragamo Museum in Florence.

This famly-run Italian conglomerate can always be found in major shopping cities around the world. →

A Centennial Exhibition
SALVATORE FERRAGAMO
THE ART OF THE SHOE

In line with its reputation of providing everything for everybody,
Beatrice Lillie once purchased an alligator
from Harrods as a Christmas present for Noel Coward;
Leka, King of Albania bought a 15-month-old, 700-pound
elephant as a gift for Governor Ronald Reagan from the store.
Which bag did it come in?

BAGTOID

Twelve million bags are
used each year, in ten
different sizes.

Harrods

For the store with the motto "Omnia Omnibus Ubique—all things, for all people, everywhere," the cable address "Everything London," and a doormat proclaiming "Enter a different world," it's no surprise that Harrods is rated the third most popular tourist attraction in London after St. Paul's Cathedral and Big Ben. In fact, there aren't many people in the world who wouldn't recognize the green-and-gold Harrods shopping bag, first created to publicize the famous Harrods sale in the mid-1930s. Legend has it that the "sale" bags were such great publicity that all people had to do was see them on the street and they would flock to Harrods for *the* sale. While the first Harrods carrier bag dates back to the 1920s raffia bag with "Harrods Poultry Department" stamped on it, since the green bag appeared, it has been around in one form or another except during World War II when retailers were not permitted by the government to waste materials on packaging. Since then other incredible bags by leading designers have been created for special promotions, some departments have their own bags, (the food hall has three), but there is still "only one Harrods" (slogan established in the 1930s) and only one green-and-gold bag (with its four Royal Warrants), officially adopted in the '70s as the main carrier bag.

Only one Harrods, in Knightsbridge.

The company moving service, Harrods Removals, inspired the advertising byline "People vote out governments, but Harrods moves in Prime Ministers." We think they move them in these bags.

BAGTOID

A GRAND TOUR OF ITALY

Harrods
KNIGHTSBRIDGE

THERE IS ONLY ONE SALE.

Harrods

Eleanor Roosevelt once wrote a letter saying
the L&T rose was the prettiest she'd ever seen.

BAGTOID

According to Lord & Taylor,
the "Star Spangled Banner"
is played at the start of each
day in all the L&T stores.
How's that for American style?

The SIGNATURE *of*
AMERICAN STYLE

Lord & Taylor

Founded in New York City in 1826, this is America's oldest specialty department store. The L&T promise—a pledge of fashion, quality, service and value—has kept this store "the signature of American style," but it's their red rose symbol that gives this store its heart and soul. Legend has it that Lord and Taylor's Dorothy Shaver, the first female president of an American department store, had her sales staff present a single rose with each purchase made. That gesture was, in turn, symbolized by the rose used for many years on the bag, now used for special promo purposes only. (If you don't have an old one, snag one of these.)

More than 50 stores across America.

Bonwit Teller/B. Altman & Company

New York shoppers still haven't gotten over the loss of these two great department stores. The lucky ones whisper, "I have a Bonwit's bag." Others reminisce, "Do you remember Altman's Christmas bag?" Mention violets to dedicated shoppers and only one image springs to mind: the Bonwit Teller shopping bag. In a class by itself, this was the unflashy, classy member of the "B" stores (Bloomingdale's, Bonwit's, Bendel's and now Barneys). While the B. Altman department store began with a 'B,' it will always be "A-number-one" on the list of deceased stores to mourn. These bags are true collectibles because there's no way to get new ones.

Chapter 6
DOGGIE BAGS

IT WAS INEVITABLE THAT THIS TREND WOULD START IN AMERICA:
FOOD AND DRINK BEING CARRIED HOME IN STYLE.
YEARS AGO IF YOU HAD THE COURAGE TO ASK
TO TAKE HOME LEFTOVERS,
AT BEST YOU'D BE PRESENTED WITH A TINFOIL SWAN.
NOW IT DOESN'T TAKE ANY COURAGE
BECAUSE DESIGNERS HAVE COME UP WITH THE ULTIMATE DOGGIE BAGS.

"One of the last places in New York that makes you
feel like dressing up."
New York Times' food critic Ruth Reichl

Tuscan Square

The man behind the success of NYC's Le Madri is the brains behind this new Rockefeller Center restaurant and shop. With the ambiance of Tuscany, it's an inviting space with delicious food and drink to please your palate and lifestyle products handpicked to turn your home into a Tuscan retreat. The bags architecturally mirror the restaurant's design.

Midtown Manhattan.

La Caravelle

The lovely setting enhanced by Jean Pagès's murals, the classic French cooking with a touch of invention and lightness, and the courteous service would make an outing to this restaurant perfect enough. But the pièce de résistance, which can be seen upon entering and exiting the restaurant, is a display of shopping bags from all over the world, placing this establishment in a category all of its own.

A little bit of France in midtown Manhattan.

"She always believed in the old adage,
leave them when your bag is full. . . ."
Anita Loos

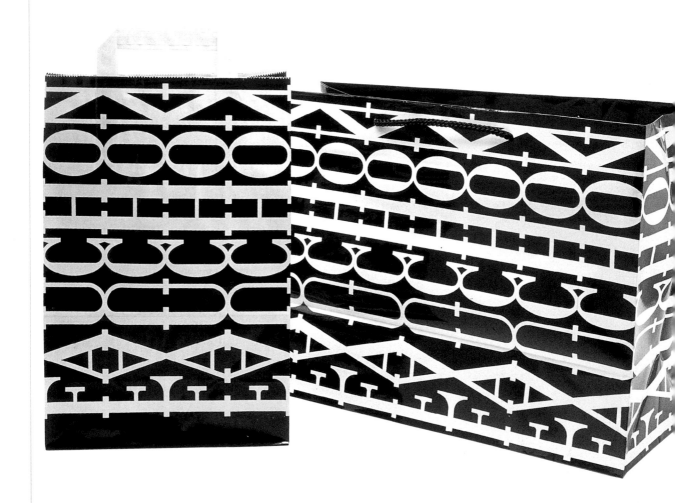

Mariage Frères

One does not automatically associate tea with France, but if you need a cup or glass or just want to buy one of more than 350 different kinds of teas or companion products, then Mariage Frères is *the* place. Established in 1854, the Mariage brothers took a leaf, so to speak, out of the Oriental book of teamaking, and elevated the provision of the popular product to an art form. One look at their logo on the bag and you know you've encountered the connoisseurs of tea. Stop by for tea and you'll be handed a menu as thick as a book, with a selection of hundreds of teas. The book suggests appropriate teas for the time of day, and the waiters fill in with further recommendations.

Three in Paris.

Fauchon

With 119 kinds of jams, 93 brands of tea, 35 types of honey, 44 sorts of mustard, 56 flavors of vinegar, 45 varieties of chocolate, Fauchon has come to epitomize French refinement and taste and not only offers the best products from France and around the world, but also displays them as works of art. For more than a century Fauchon has been located on Paris's Place de la Madeleine and has been known as the "retail museum of food." Although the bag is not edible, we think it's a work of art too.

Only one Fauchon, but sales outlets in 32 countries.

"Retail is detail." Howard Schultz, CEO, Starbucks

Known for its nouvelle cuisine,
not much of it usually leaves the premises, despite the
bag. (Le Cirque 2000)

BAGTOID More than 5 million people visit a
Starbucks location each week.

DEAN & DELUCA

Dean & DeLuca: Once the first store opened in New York City, gourmet food buying, shopping, browsing, and eating would never be the same. There are aisles upon aisles of select things you never knew you wanted until you saw it here. And D&D has just the right bag to bring it all home in. Although the bag was designed in 1977 (by Jack Ceglic), the year this first store opened, it hasn't changed since. "It feels clean and fresh as the food," says owner Georgio DeLuca about the bag. He's right about the bag and he's right about the food.

← New York, Washington, D.C., Charlotte, and North Carolina.

Le Cirque 2000: Adam Tihany's design of "Jetsons meet Buckingham Palace decor"(*New York Post*) has orbited Sirio Maccioni's legendary restaurant into the 21st century. Now ensconced in NYC's elegant Villiard House, the food and decor are equally astonishing. The only low-key thing about the entire experience of dining here is their timeless doggie bag—connecting high society's favorite haunt with its new headquarters.

←

Starbucks: This American institution, started in Seattle's Pike Place Market in 1971, is named for "Starbuck" the first mate in Herman Melville's classic novel *Moby Dick*. Since then, it has become North America's leading retailer, roaster, and brand of specialty coffee. Inspired by the number of espresso bars in Italy, Starbucks is rapidly expanding into the Pacific Rim and in Europe, giving people a place where they can hang out. The distinctively designed bags are good to hang onto too and are almost as recognizable as one from McDonald's.

← Across North America, Japan, Hawaii, Singapore, and the
Philippines. Soon to wake up people everywhere.

"Papa's gotta brand new bag. . . ,"
as the granddaddy of them all.
James Brown, sings. . . .

"An empty shopping bag cannot stand upright."
Benjamin Franklin

The cerise and orange bag designed by Serendipity's owner
Stephen Bruce in the '60s showed that small was great and
the more outrageous the color the better. Yves Saint Laurent
obviously agreed.

Planet Hollywood:
Cranking up the HRC theme to the
next level, Planet Hollywood realized
that their customers wanted more.
They needed constant visual stimula-
tion along with their taste sensation.
So Hollywood stars, among them,
Arnie, Bruce, and Sly, became partners and welcomed ordinary folk into
their orbit. Naturally they are hos-
pitable enough to offer us the
opportunity to take home some of
their aura in this bright plastic bag.

Eighty-seven restaurants on Planet Earth.

Motown Cafe: Give the rock'n'roll
that distinct Detroit sound, change
the food to soul, and it spells the
popular M-O-T-O-W-N C-A-F-E.

Growing fast.

Serendipity: Decorated like an old-
fashioned general store, there isn't
another restaurant like this in New
York, and, aside from the chains,
this is where kids love to come.
Everywhere you look there are deco-
rations on the walls, but it's the
frozen hot chocolate drinks and foot-
long hot dogs that get the kids' vote,
not to mention the great gifts you
can buy to put into the special shopping bags.

Only one on Manhattan's Upper East Side.

Chapter 7
DESIGN FOR LIVING

LIVING IS EASY WHEN YOU KNOW YOUR LIFESTYLE.
BE IT MODERN. TRADITIONAL.
SHABBY CHIC AND/OR ECLECTIC.
THERE'S A STYLE OR TWO FOR EVERYONE.
FROM THE HUNT FOR THE PERFECT DOORKNOB
TO A ROAD MAP OF THE HOW-TO WORLD OF DECORATING.
THESE BAGS BRING IT ON HOME.
MAKING YOUR PERSONAL NEST YOUR VERY OWN DESIGN FOR LIVING.

BAGTOID Only one of eight companies bearing the four Royal Warrants of the Queen, the Queen Mother, Prince Philip, and Prince Charles. Could that be the reason Fergie and Andrew registered for wedding gifts here? Or was it the bag?

EST **GTC** 1920
THE GENERAL TRADING COMPANY
SLOANE SQUARE
LONDON

ARGYLE STREET BATH

Jerry's Home Store

From those Nestlés tollhouse chocolate chips to the latest in barbecue
equipment, Jerry's Home Store has
become the houseware-away-from-
home store for Americans. Even if
you aren't American (and surprisingly the owner isn't), it's the store to
shop in London with a distinct New
York point of view. Started five years
ago on London's fashionable Fulham
Road, there are now three more
stores, with others soon to open in
major cities across Europe. Maybe
that's why the carrier bag has been
changed from blue with a white logo
to an even more appropriate design—
Uncle Sam's stars and stripes.

Fulham Road, Hampstead, Harvey Nichols, and Surrey.

The General Trading Co.

Founded in 1920 by Colonel Dealtry
Part, this family-owned shop selling
household goods was one of the first
to offer bridal registry services in the
UK. One step into the store and we'd
sign up immediately. The store is
filled with must-haves; every nook
and cranny has something you'd
want to buy whether it's antiques,
china, glassware, table linens, lamps,
or stationery. As much thought was
put into the design of the store's logo,
created in 1959 by Tom Wolsey, then
the art director at Conde Nast. The
1930s Bauhaus symbols of the
square, triangle, and circle are used,
neatly accommodating the company's
three initials.

London with branches in Bath and Cirencester.

colette
styledesignartfood

colette

Like Paris's other famed Colette, this store is the most talked about in the fashion capital, and everyone is trying to figure out just what this boutique is all about. As *Travel and Leisure* put it, "Seldom have so few things attracted so much attention." It's a one-stop shop—styledesignartfood. Everything for the millennium and all meticulously planned, from the product to the weekly changed display. The downstairs "water bar" offers 40 different kinds of water, and according to Sarah, comanager of the store, "It is one of the few places in Paris where you can eat lunch whenever you want." The clever logo—white with two dots—changes color with the seasons and appears on all the bags and some of the merchandise too. There's only one colette—that in itself makes the store and its bag irresistible.

Paris, two blocks from the Ritz.

"The design of the Octopus logo takes on a slight abstraction,
so not to tie the company concept down to one school of thought.
The colors and shape used in the carrier bag design enable the logo to be easily reconizable,
giving the company a strong and distinctive corporate image.
Hopefully in the future to be as identifiable as the kick logo used by Nike."
Owner, Octopus.

Octopus

Here's a shopping bag created to "carry" customers to the store. One look at this bag and you just have to find this store to see what is sold. Once you get there, you're still not sure, but you can have a great time discovering all sorts of things—bags disguised as animals, umbrellas as tulips, rubber gloves glamorous enough to wear anywhere inside and outside of the home. Born on a barrow in the King's Walk Mall on Kings Road, London in 1994 (the store, not the octopus), the aim of the owners was "to create a unique brand of accessories and interiors known for intelligent design and humor." Not only have they succeeded, but they are creating new branches and will soon have more stores than an octopus has tentacles.

Five stores in the UK, three in London.

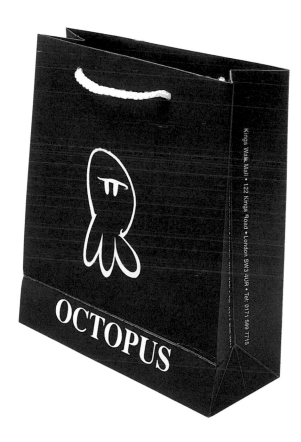

Kings Walk Mall • 122 Kings Road • London SW3 4UR • Tel: 0171 589 7715

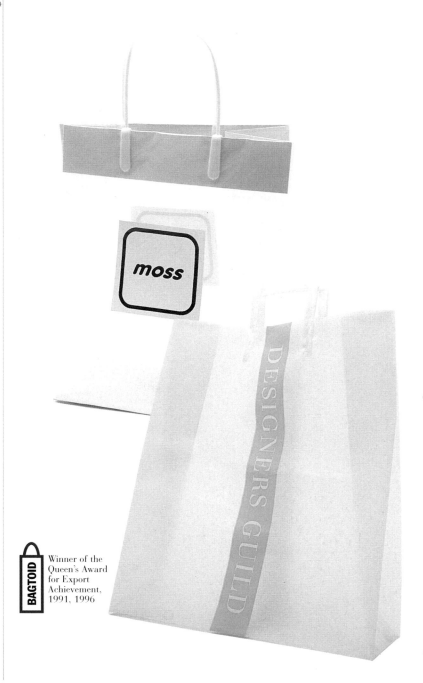

BAGTOID Winner of the Queen's Award for Export Achievement, 1991, 1996

Moss

Murray Moss's vision has come to life in the center of NYC's Soho. It's an homage to modern design and decorative arts in the shape of a store that looks just like an art gallery. Opened in 1994, its 20th-century wares are all displayed in glass cases—a theme that is carried through in every aspect—right down to the see-through shopping bags enabling consumers to display the products even after purchasing them.

Soho, New York

Designers Guild

If you like your color palette bold and beautiful, then the Designers Guild is a must. Started by Trisha Guild, author of eight books on color and design, the Designers Guild's range is so broad that it encompasses more than 2,000 fabrics and 600 wallpapers, classical and contemporary upholstered furniture, bed and bath linens, towels, china, and table settings, not to mention a children's line, toys, and accessories in all shapes, sizes, and, of course, colors. The bag is just as colorful.

Retail showrooms in London, Paris, and Munich.

Maxim's

The boutique of the famous restaurant, which features in the opera *The Merry Widow*, is still located at its legendary address at 3 rue Royale and now owned by Pierre Cardin. Although the restaurant has a hard act to follow living up to its illustrious past, the boutique does not disappoint, selling all sorts of objects that help to re-create the illusion of past grandeur, just like its shopping bag with its famous painting by Sem, one of the artists of the années folles.

Paris, 3 rue Royale.

Sentou Galerie

The store is almost as colorful in temperament and modern in feel as its bags. Everything for the home as long as your interest is contemporary—from designers as distinct as Noguchi to Aalto. A word to the wise—leave your shopping bags at the desk; even the best-intentioned customer can cause a breakable crash in the aisles surrounded by fragile glass. And a special thanks to the management with the capability of shrugging it off gracefully.

Two stores in Paris.

BAGTOID The design of the bag is based on the Eugenie & Bordure fabric (the store's best-selling) which was rejuvenated from an 18th-century shawl.

Pierre Deux

If you can't get to Provence, the next best thing is to go to Pierre Deux, the French country home furnishings shop specializing in fabrics, 18th-century antique and reproduction furniture, pewter, table furnishings, and all those household accessories that are oh, so French. It's impossible to leave without being color coordinated and without at least one of their exquisite shopping bags (and boxes).

Atlanta, Beverly Hills, Boston, Carmel, Dallas, New York, Palm Beach, San Francisco, Winnetka, and Tokyo.

MacKenzie-Childs

Through a looking glass. One glance at MacKenzie-Childs's shopping bag and you must see more. A doorman with a top hat opens the door, and pheasants greet each new visitor, as a medley of offbeat and exquisite household furnishings in polka dots, ocher, terracotta, squiggly lines, bursts of colors and shapes immediately captures the imagination. Each new floor, each new room, is a different world. Even the most miserly, miserable shopper must smile, particularly if an upside-downside tea on the top floor is included in the tour. This store is one-of-a-kind, as is its bag. Frame it. But get two because the illustration on each side is different.

Madison Avenue, New York.

Czech & Speake

Like the subtle black, white and grey spotted pattern on its carrier bag, Czech & Speake, the Edwardian-inspired bathroom specialist, exudes simplicity, elegance, and innovation. From taps to fragrances, robes to towels, this store is an Anglophile's dream, as is its bag.

Two stores in London, one on that most English Street—Jermyn.

ABC Carpet & Home

It all began in 1897 when Sam Weinrib, a newly arrived Austrian immigrant, began to sell used carpet and linoleum from a pushcart on Manhattan's Lower East Side. His son turned the pushcart into a store, and now the fourth generation has masterminded its expansion into one of the leading stores for furniture, antiques, textiles, accessories, and, of course, rugs. Occupying 350,000 square feet of selling space, 200,000 square feet of warehouse with more than 900 employees, the store is visited by more than one million customers a year. With the ambience of a market, a country antiques fair, a Middle Eastern bazaar, and an endless attic filled with treasures, it is no wonder that the ABC philosophy is "collect, don't decorate." The bags fit right into that philosophy which is as perfect as "ABC."

Manhattan's Flatiron district, Bronx Warehouse, Delray Beach, Florida, and Westbury, New York.

A real find for anyone's collection: Czech & Speake's Christmas purple-and-white-flaked bag. Even we don't have one.

BAGTOID

Scalamandré: Designs, manufactures, and markets wholesale and custom-ordered, woven and printed fabrics, wallcoverings, trimmings, and carpets. Their work can be seen in the finest homes around the world—including the White House, where they've been involved in every President's historical restoration since that of Herbert Hoover. Scalamandré is open to the trade only. But don't let that deter you from trying to obtain this precious shopping bag. If you can't afford to cover your walls with their wares, at least you can prominently display the bag featuring the Jubilee fabric in your living room.

Showrooms around the U.S.

Not surprisingly, the world of high-end interior design is responsible for the most beautiful carrier bags.

These are three of the loveliest:

Scalamandré
Osborne & Little
Old World Weavers

Osborne & Little: Osborne & Little is a British design firm that specializes in fabrics and carpets. Peter Osborne and Anthony Little started the company in London's Chelsea in 1968, determined to bring imagination and color into the staid world of home decorating. Judging from these bags, they've succeeded.

Distribution worldwide 63 countries.

Old World Weavers: With a 55-year-old history as a leading textile source, Old World Weavers is a veritable archive for designers, architects, curators, and students. One look at the bag, designed by Iris Apfel, the company's founder and former owner, and you understand why Stark Carpet Corporation bought them.

Headquarters at the Decoration and Design (D&D) Building with showrooms in 30 cities.

The Conran Shop

Sir Terence Conran was one of the first to take modern international design in home fashion and make it accessible to middle class modern living. More than two decades strong, The Conran Shop is alive and thriving in London with a new store opened in 1997 at Marylebone. But it was the move to the Michelin House that triggered the current carrier bag design. James Pylott, graphic designer in the Conran Design Group, was inspired by a painting he saw in a magazine and came up with the concept which was interpreted and painted by Sian Tucker.

London (two stores), Paris, and Tokyo. →

Mulberry

Ironically, the label most associated with English country living began on a kitchen table in a London flat, where Roger Saul started designing leather chokers and belts more than 25 years ago. Today the entire range extends from its famous leather goods to clothing to home fashion, with stores in the world's major cities. Even if you are not a "To the Manor Born" wannabe, you will want this richly designed shopping bag, not to mention Mulberry's special annual home collection carrier bag. It's enough to drive you to huntin', shootin' and fishin' (the theme for its signature Mulberry leather accessories).

In more than 15 countries with boutiques in major department stores. →

Chapter 8
THESE ARE KIDDIE BAGS

EVERY PARENT KNOWS YOU CAN'T HIDE THESE BAGS FROM YOUR KIDS.
THEY KNOW WHAT'S INSIDE IS FOR THEM ONLY.
FROM THE FINEST TOYS IN THE WORLD TO THE ULTIMATE PLAYGROUND.
WITH STOPS IN BETWEEN FOR MINI FASHIONS.
THESE ARE FUN BAGS. THESE ARE HAPPY BAGS.
THESE ARE HOPEFULLY TANTRUM-FREE BAGS. THESE ARE KIDDIE BAGS.

Founder William Hamley
called it "Noah's Ark."

Hamleys/FAO Schwarz

You don't have to buy anything to
have fun in these stores. But if you're
a kid, after playing around there's
nothing like leaving with one of these
bags filled with a new toy.

Hamleys: Founded in 1760, Hamleys
is the biggest name in toy stores, and
its seven floors with 30,000 square
feet provide room for every toy fantasy and delight. You can even rent a
section of the store for evening parties
for those who just can't stop playing.

Only one in London.

FAO Schwarz: Electric trains, life-
size animals, a Barbie boutique, the
latest games, one of the most popular
destinations for tourists and New
Yorkers alike. No wonder the films
Big and *Home Alone 2* made it a star-
ring attraction.

New York City and other American cities.

Bonpoint sells 10 percent of the French population's wedding and funeral clothing. Started by two sisters in 1972, Bonpoint has many points—shoes, furniture, men's clothes, women's clothes.

BAGTOID

Design: de Studio bv for Olly's bv/Oilily

Oilily/OshKosh B'Gosh

Before Gap Kids (was there a before Gap Kids?), there was a simple time when boys wore baby blue and girls frilly pink. Those days are gone, thanks to these two distinct stores. Their brilliant splashy colors with bold designs and hip cuts made it fun to dress like a kid. One look at these bags and you just have to smile.

OshKosh B'Gosh: Fifth Avenue, New York City, USA, Continental Europe.   Oilily: Dutch chain store with locations worldwide.

Bonpoint

Bonpoint is the French dress-up heaven for children. Organza dresses, bonnets, matching shoes, and socks. The kind of clothes a kid just has to be good in. Not that there aren't "child-friendly" clothes for everyday (for every age group, boys and girls), but even those are special. Just as is the bag. Bonbag.

Paris (15 stores), New York, London, Brussels, Geneva, Milan, Rome, Madrid, and Barcelona.

Chapter 9
PAPER BAG WRITERS

WHILE A BLANK SHEET OF PAPER IS A WRITER'S WORST NIGHTMARE.
THESE BAGS FILL UP EASILY.
FROM ORDINARY TO EXTRAORDINARY IMPLEMENTS OF THE TRADE.
FROM ART BOOKS AND FICTION TO COFFEE(TABLE)
AND DISCOUNT BOOKS. THESE ARE THE PAPER BAG WRITERS.

Ordning & Reda

As innovative as these bags are with their bold graphic design, so are the stores which are located in 12 countries. What makes this Swedish stationery store unique is that its wide range of products are designed by one company only, are handmade, and environmentally friendly. Only a Swede could come up with such a variety of coordinated cards, papers, boxes, folders, notebooks, diaries, address books, portfolios, binders, magazine collectors, spiral pads, photo albums, guest books, scrapbooks, drawing blocks, note pads, wrapping papers, note cards, and writing papers, as well as almost 300 associated products such as bags and pens. It must be those long cold winters.

Sweden, Denmark, Norway, England, Switzerland, Austria, France, Netherlands, Belgium, Germany, Japan, and the U.S.

The latest Smythson must-have is a "little pink book" (the female equivalent of the little black book). Waiting lists everywhere.

Smythson

"Renowned for our bespoke stationery" states Symthson's, adding in their understated British manner, "Most likely the best personalised stationery in the world." Founded in 1887 by silversmith Frank Smythson, the store now holds three Royal Warrants and made global news in 1953 when Sir Edmund Hillary conquered Mt. Everest carrying a Smythson featherweight diary. He might just have easily been carrying a Smythson shopping bag because it's just as durable and recognizable as a symbol of British class and style. The bag is made of Smythson watermarked Nile blue writing paper milled in Scotland, the color inspired by a trip the founder made to Egypt. Today, whether carried across the desert or to the top of a mountain or by Madonna as she walks down fashionable Bond Street, everyone knows this remarkable bag.

London's fashionable New Bond and Sloan Streets, Harvey Nichols, and Heathrow Airport.

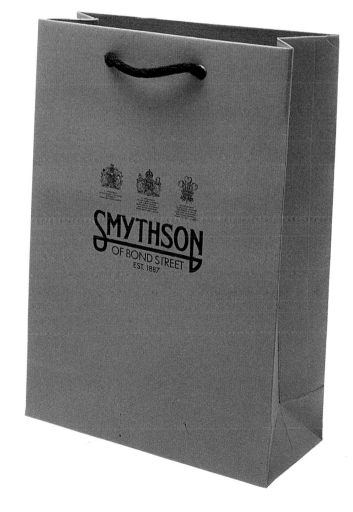

Rizzoli/Barnes & Noble/Borders Books & Music

Competition in the world of bookselling has created wonderful
new features like easy chairs, cafés, and readings.

The bags of each of these bookstores are as distinctive as the stores
themselves.

"We're trying to build a global brand.
It's an adult playground."
Robert DiRomuardo, CEO, Borders

Rizzoli: Has the feel and look of an old-world library specializing in the arts and foreign languages. A wonderful store to browse and to buy in. The bag is as old world as the store.

Fifteen stores in the U.S.

Barnes & Noble: The King of book stores, this is a place where people love to linger. The discounts are appealing; the relaxed ambience with overstuffed chairs and a café encourage you to stay; and the bags prove that a picture is still worth a thousand words.

All over the U.S.

Borders Books & Music: Borders has it all, just like Barnes & Noble started it all, and has a deep list and knowledgeable staff. Now they have expanded their U.S. operation and have gone global, taking their customer-friendly service to England, Scotland, Australia, and Singapore, proving there are no borders.

Where the best books are sold—including this one.

Chapter 10
BAGS FOR ART'S SAKE

WHEN THE MUSEUM WORLD REALIZED
THAT ART NEEDED TO MEET THE WORLD OF MARKETING
TO SURVIVE (AND THRIVE),
EVERYTHING CHANGED: FROM MEMBERSHIPS
TO BLOCKBUSTER EXHIBITIONS TO CORPORATE
FUNDING TO MUSEUM SHOPS SELLING
ANYTHING EVEN REMOTELY RELATED.
WHO WOULD HAVE THOUGHT SO MANY PEOPLE WOULD WALK AROUND WITH...
BAGS FOR ART'S SAKE?

Design by Stuart Silver

Courtesy Art Dealers' Association of America Henry Street Settlement

The Art Show

What started as a benefit by the Art Dealers' Association for the Henry Street Settlement House in 1989, has quickly become an annual February international event. With art from all periods displayed, more than 12,000 people enter the historic doors of the Park Avenue Armory each year. This bag advertising the logo of the show, however, was a one-time only, marking the debut year. Bring back the bag.

The Armory, Park Avenue, New York City.

Cooper-Hewitt National Design Museum
Smithsonian Institution

Inspired by Paris's Musée des Arts Décoratifs and London's Victoria & Albert Museum, the Cooper Union Museum for the Arts and Decoration was founded in 1897 in New York by three granddaughters of industrialist Peter Cooper. In 1967 the collections of the Museum were transferred to the Smithsonian Institution and found a new home in the Andrew Carnegie Mansion in New York. Housed in what was once the music room, the Cooper-Hewitt store is about as eclectic a museum boutique as anyone could wish for, only selling the most innovative of designed objects and books relating to the museum's exhibitions. The bag is more than appropriately designed.

At the museum on Fifth Avenue at 91st Street, New York.

The centennial shopping bag was
designed by Douglas Riccardi
of Memo Productions, Inc., inspired
by the Fifth Avenue
signage created for the Museum
by its Adjunct Curator of
Contemporary Design, Ellen Lupton.
The circles can be read as confetti or
balloons, appropriate for a birthday party.
Each contains a fact about the Museum's
history, collections, staff, programs,
mission, or physical facility—the Carnegie
mansion and its garden. The choice
of typefaces and the use of highly
keyed colors against a field of white
project a forward-looking profile
for a Museum founded in
the Victorian era,
more than 100 years ago.

BAGTOID

The Museum of Modern Art (MoMA)/
Solomon R. Guggenheim Museum/
The Metropolitan Museum of Art

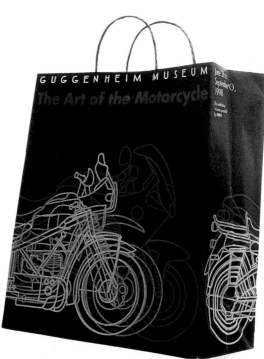

The Museum of Modern Art (MoMA): Founded in 1929 by three wealthy art collectors, MoMA was originally housed in six rooms in an office building at 57th and Fifth. It became the first international collection of modern art in the world and is considered by many to have the most comprehensive collection of 20th-century art. The selection of art books in its store is second to none and the objects on sale in its design store define good design. So does the classic MoMA shopping bag.

Bookstore—11 West 53rd Street; Design Store—44 West 53rd Street, New York.

Solomon R. Guggenheim Museum, NY: Designed by Frank Lloyd Wright, the Guggenheim is the youngest building to be designated a NYC landmark. Also housed within its walls is the Guggenheim Museum store where a purchase will give you a work of art to take home—the shopping bag.

Fifth Avenue and Soho, NY; Venice; Bilbao, Spain; and Berlin.

The Metropolitan Museum of Art: As fresh as it was when it first appeared in the late 1970s, the head-turning shopping bag from the Metropolitan Museum of Art has become an American icon. Rudy De Harak's award-winning design for the bag was introduced to coincide with the opening of the new Art Publication Center, now known as the bookshop off the Museum's Great Hall. Its three bold colors—blue, yellow, and red—represent the elemental pigments for color printing: cyan, yellow, and magenta.

Met Museum stores: Costa Mesa, Century City, Pasadena, CA; Denver, CO; Farmington, CT; Stamford, CT; Atlanta; Short Hills, N.J.; Manhasset, NY; The Cloisters; Macy's Herald Square; The Metropolitan Museum of Art; Rockefeller Center; Soho, NY; Columbus, OH; Houston, TX; Switzerland, France, Mexico, Japan, Hong Kong, Singapore, and Manila.

(The Met) More than one million bags are printed every year, making it one of the most visible symbols of the largest repository of art in the Western hemisphere. Won the American Institute of Graphic Arts Award (AIGA).

BAGTOID The image on the Rodin Museum's transparent carrier bag is a portrait of Rodin by Henri Dornac taken from an old photograph belonging to the Museum archive.

Rodin Museum

When the wealthy financier Abraham Peyrenc de Moras dreamt of building the finest house in Paris in 1728, even he could not have possibly envisioned that Rodin's "The Thinker" would someday live there. The mansion had a lively history, but it wasn't until 1904 when the property became the residence of artists such as Isadora Duncan, Cocteau, Matisse, Rilke, and Rodin, that the mansion was not only saved from being demolished, but bought by the French government who convinced Rodin to donate his collections to the state. The doors opened in 1919 and the public can now enjoy one of the "finest houses in Paris" with no doubt one of the greatest collections of sculpture and art. The Museum store's bag is also one of the greatest.

Paris and Mendon, France.

The Louvre

This is a museum you can get lost in for days, particularly since I. M. Pei's glass pyramid not only transformed the site, but doubled the exhibition space. Like Paris, the museum is divided into arrondissements and also like the capital city it is best to roam and take in the beauty. The carrier bag says it all—with the Louvre floating in the soft pink clouds on top of one of the world's metropolitan wonders.

Paris, where else?

Victoria & Albert Museum

Founded by Prince Albert in the 1850s as the Museum of Manufactures, it wasn't until 1899 when Queen Victoria laid the foundation stone that the Museum received its current name. Little did Prince Albert know when orders were given to confine the museum's purchases "to objects where Fine Art is applied to some purpose of utility," that today it would house everything from the Raphael Cartoons to Salvador Dali's lipstick pink sofas in the shape of one of Mae West's kisses to Reeboks. But the true star is the mosaic carrier bag with the purple handles and lining.

London.

National Gallery

Created in 1824 when George IV persuaded the government to purchase 38 paintings, the National Gallery in London now has more than 2,000 works of art from the 13th through the 20th centuries, representing virtually every major school. While the visitor can view any painting or sculpture by touching a screen at the Micro Gallery, the bookstore has an incredible assortment of museum-related products to bring home. Best are the carrier bags—the generic ones designed by Susan Gilson at National Gallery Productions Ltd, and the ones for special exhibitions.

London.

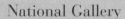

SPANISH STILL LIFE
from Velázquez to Goya

THE NATIONAL GALLERY   22 February – 21 May 1995   Sponsored by *Glaxo*

Christie's

Founded in 1766, Christie's has been a fine arts auctioneer for more than 200 years. With principal selling centers in New York and London, regular auctions are also held in the leading capitals of the world in approximately 80 categories from fine and applied arts and collectibles to wine and cars. Not only does Christie's undertand what the public wants, they undestand what they want to collect—from rare events such as the auction of Nureyev's estate in 1995 (which included not only art and sculpture but a harpsichord and ballet boots) and Princess Di's dresses in 1997 (including creations from Victor Edelstein, Gina Fratini, and Catherine Walker). We wouldn't part with the bags—even at an auction.

Major capitals of the world.

Sotheby's

From its first auction of books in 1744 for a few hundred pounds, this British auction house has become not just one of the oldest, but the largest fine and decorative arts auctioneers in the world. The variety of what passes under the hammer today can only amaze—from racing cars to Russian space capsules, to teddy bears, to Napoleon's books, to the most famous paintings and sculptures in the world. While auctions can be great social events, the public viewing before a sale can be staggering. The lines to view the Duchess of Windsor's jewels before the auction were blocks long.

Major capitals of the world.

Chapter 11
ONE-OF-A-KIND BIDDING BAGS

ONE HAD JACKIE, ONE HAD DI.
THEY BOTH KNEW THE "RULES OF THE GAME."
JUST AS HIGH ROLLERS AT CHRISTIE'S AND SOTHEBY'S DO.
IT'S THE FINE ART OF SHOPPING,
BEST DONE WITH A POKER FACE
BECAUSE ONLY THE BIDDER KNOWS THE LIMITS,
BUT IF YOU DON'T WANT TO PLAY,
BUY A CATALOGUE AND YOU TOO CAN OBTAIN
ONE-OF-A-KIND BIDDING BAGS.

Paul Dyson, Design Department, Sotheby's London

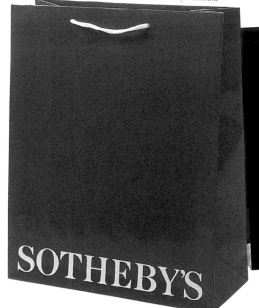

CHRISTIE'S
ART

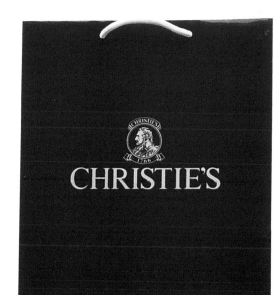

CHRISTIE'S

DRESSES

CHRISTIE'S

NUREYEV

CHRISTIE'S

Chapter 12
ALL THAT GLITTERS

THESE BAGS HOLD PROMISE.
THEY ARE SPECIAL-OCCASION BAGS.
(ISN'T EVERY DAY A SPECIAL-OCCASION DAY?)
NO MATTER WHAT'S INSIDE.
EVERYONE WANTS ALL THAT GLITTERS.

"Absent by design. With an elite international clientele of heads of state, film stars, captains of industry, privacy is of the utmost importance. Clients are never disclosed and to further maintain their privacy, the Harry Winston tote bag was purposely designed to be inconspicuous. The firm's clients do not need or want to flaunt their purchase, and the famed jeweler itself is secure with the simple fact that its deep blue bags sans logo carry the rarest jewels in the world."

So Harry Winston replied when we requested a bag and the store asked that we run this copy instead inside an empty, colorless shopping bag. We'd probably prefer the jewels too.

Lisa Maria Presley's summation of her experiences
on a photo shoot for the book *Untamed* by Cartier says it all.

"I experienced criminal impulses while wearing the jewels.
I wanted to try and run for the hills,
but the jewels' bodyguards outnumbered my own."

Luckily she didn't try it. She wouldn't get far carrying this bag!

Right: White bag designed for
Cartier's 150th anniversary

Cartier

Despite its ethereal white aura and rich, deep red hues, these are no fantasy bags. Every piece of jewelry here is real, running the gamut from the elegantly tasteful signature pieces to the rocks that will knock the socks off even the most jaded shoppers. In its 150 years, Cartier has bejeweled most luminaries. Let's not forget Elizabeth Taylor's 69-carat diamond birthday present from Richard Burton.

Everywhere you'd like to be.

"Our shopping bags reflect
the Judith Leiber collection.
They are both designed with the finest
quality materials."
Judith Leiber, public relations

Judith Leiber is a registered trademark of Time Products, Inc.

LALAoUNIS

Ilias Lalaounis's designs bring the art of past civilizations into the present. Every creation is a treasure, whether it be inspired from an actual treasure (of Troy) or from the Mycenaean art spiral motif symbolizing eternity. The bag is a treasure, too. Rectangular in shape, the bags are in a shade of deep burgundy, the color prevalent in the Palace of King Minos (1800–1200 BC). In the center of the bag rests the oval logo, known as the Lalaounis "egg," which was used to enclose his Greek initials because it symbolizes life and creation.

Athens (seven shops), Corfu, Mykonos, Rhodes, Paris, Geneva, Zurich, London, New York, Tokyo, and Cyprus.

Judith Leiber

Her handbags are seen only at the most exclusive black-tie affairs, proudly carried by the ladies of society and often copied by those who can't afford the real thing. Ms. Leiber has designed more than four thousand handbags during her illustrious career, which began when she realized that women were carrying solid gold evening bags and that she could save them the time of going back and forth to the vaults before and after each affair. She came up with the idea of rhinestones on brass and "a fashion legend was born." She skyrocketed to fame in the early '70s after Greta Garbo bought her snake purse at Bergdorf's and the snake became Leiber's signature—and her good-luck charm. Not only is it printed on every shopping bag, but it's used as the wallpaper in her powder room.

Winds up at only the best places.

Mikimoto

Kokichi Mikimoto's father owned a noodle shop. He sold vegetables at the age of 13 and had a rudimentary education. Yet somehow, Mikimoto became the first man to develop a technique for the cultivation of pearls, created a company that celebrated its centenary in 1993, and gave Japan one of its first successful export products. The bag, like the Mikimoto pearl, exudes deep luster and extraordinary color.

Tokyo, London, New York, and Paris.

Tiffany & Co.

The classic robin's-egg–blue bag proves that bigger is not always better. In fact, the store was launched with a thousand dollar loan in 1837 at 259 Broadway. Following the philosophy of its founder, Charles Lewis Tiffany, it moved in 1940 into a handsome building on 57th and Fifth Avenue designed by Cross & Cross, where it continued to offer the most elegant and classic jewelry, crystal, and other luxury items. When Tiffany & Co. celebrated its bejeweled 150th anniversary in 1987, Audrey Hepburn summed it up for all of us when she wrote in a preface to the book *Tiffany's 150 Years* by John Loring: "Happy birthday dear T., with love, but also with envy, for after 150 years you don't have a wrinkle, but then, class doesn't age."

Tiffany & Co. retains its prestigious address in New York City at 57th Street and Fifth Avenue. There are more than 100 stores nationwide, but only one blue bag.

"Good design is good business." Thomas J. Watson of IBM

Above, right: Earlier version of the "world's most famous blue bag."
Copyright and Trademark Tiffany and Company

Chapter 13
BEAUTY BAGS

MAKE UP. MAKE OVER. MAKE BELIEVE.
WHEN YOU NEED A LIFT (PRE-FACE).
NOTHING SEDUCES YOUR SENSES MORE THAN
THE MAGIC POTENTS FOUND IN THESE BEAUTY BAGS.

"The basic style of the bag has not changed over the last 25 years
- to create a carrier bag which is both functional and minimal, yet
subtle in design, while tactile and touchable.
The final design reflects a simple elegance which is both
contemporary and classic. The corporate logo and cotton fabric
handles follow the black and cream brand identity with a 24-hour
iconic flower stamped in silver. The bag is redesigned every three
to four years, to ensure that it remains a modern reflection of
Molton Brown's contemporary position in the market."

Molton Brown

Begun as a '70s hairdressing salon on
South Molton Street, its name is part
street (Molton), part sister-store
(Brown's). A pioneer of the 'natural
beauty look,' this was the first British
cosmetics company to list contents on
packaging, and still makes its products by hand, rather than machine.
With its lipstick selected by the San
Francisco Museum of Modern Art as
an icon for the '90s depicting the
marriage between function and form,
it is also chosen by lots of celebs,
such as Tom Cruise, Nicole Kidman.
Cher, Bruce Willis, Stephanie Seymour and, of course, Madonna (how
does she fit it all in?). Molton Brown
cosmetics also star in America's TV
series *Melrose Place*, and were
among the first to be distributed by
airlines in-flight. Hope they use the
bag—it's great!

Distributed in 41 countries.

Space NK: Space for, well—space, NK for owner Nicky Kinnaird who has revolutionized beauty product shopping. Not only has she come up with a solution to that confusing department store experience of aisles vs. aisles of competing products, but she has simplified the search for cutting-edge cosmetics by doing it for us. The carrier bags and color chart envelopes are just as innovative.

Six locations in London, mail order catalogue. →

M.A.C.: Make-up Art Cosmetics, a Canadian company launched for professionals, famed for its lip colors (140, but the favorite is still spice) and yes, make-overs, is still considered hip as is its transparent bag. Founded in 1985 when the Canadian makeup artist Frank Toskan couldn't find the colors he wanted and got his brother-in-law with a bent for chemistry to start mixing in the kitchen. The results are on the faces of celebrities such as Madonna (where does she get the time?) and in the sales (Estée Lauder now owns 51 percent of the company). With k.d. lang and drag queen RuPaul as the current M.A.C. faces, they are covering all the bases. Even better is the philosophy—recycled packaging (return six empty lipsticks and you get one free) and contributions (2 million dollars to AIDS research).

In every pro's makeup case. →

"Space NK carrier bags and cosmetic envelopes were designed to reflect the products they carry. The outer of the carrier bags is designed around the optimum shape and size to fit small heavy items. The outside of the carrier reflects a feeling of calm and restraint while the inside reveals silver fingerprints to convey the customer's reaction—one of a 'kid in a candy store.' The colour chart envelopes relate to the rainbow of colours available within the store."

Why RuPaul is such a good choice as promoter for M.A.C.:
"No one wears as much makeup as me."
RuPaul

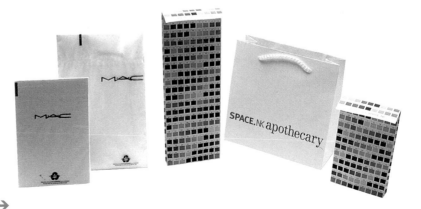

"An outer packaging today is your means of advertising, a walking advertisement which acts as a window to your product. There are two things we look for in our outer packaging. It must represent the product to the full with the same standards of quality on everything from paper and print to the handle. Do not cut corners on costings. Also packaging must have longevity and the ability to be used more than once." Jo Malone

"I always use perfume where I expect to be kissed."
Coco Chanel

"Years ago, women perceived beauty as a luxury and frivolous. . . . The British woman is starting to see beauty with different eyes, as a necessity instead of a luxury." Jo Malone, *Allure*, 1998

Penhaligon's/
Annick Goutal Parfum/
Jo Malone

Annick Goutal Parfum: This former concert pianist turned her talent to another sense when she began to create subtle, delicate scents in 1981. Her light touch caresses the vision as well, with its fluttery ivory and gold packaging and displays. In fact, it is so effervescent that the company has since been bought out by champagne maker Tattinger, leaving the expert in charge of creation. The clientele is just as impressive as the bag. Madonna uses Passion (when does she sleep?), and Prince Charles, Eau d'Hadrien.

Paris.

Jo Malone: Jo Malone's love affair with scent dates back to the age of seven when she remembers filling tiny bottles with fragrant smelling rose petals. At twenty she went to the center of the world of fragrance—Grasse—to study with the "top noses." Back in England she developed her own line of beauty products and a client list so long that by 1994 she just *had* to open her first shop. Her perfume line started as gifts for her clients, but as the demand grew so did the business. Today her products are sold in London, New York, and Paris and by mail—"Sent-a-Scent." As if this success weren't enough, Jo Malone continues to pioneer new uses for her scents, creating a fragrance for McDonald's hand wipes and a bath line for French Connection. Now she's started a new business called "Scent an Event." What could be next?

London, Paris (Joseph Shop), New York (Bergdorf Goodman).

Penhaligon's: Begun in 1870 by a barber and apothecary, the Penhaligon's product is known primarily for its vintage and newly invented English scents. Still available is Winston Churchill's favorite, Blenheim Bouquet, whose mixture of confidence and discretion he found specially appealing, and their first scent for women, Lily of the Valley, which designer Tricia Guild wears (see Designers Guild). Then there's Cornubia which carries a scent of wanton seductiveness and the distinct reputation, if worn, for rarely getting past the first course. And, Hamman Bouquet (created in 1872), which Franco Zeffirelli took a bottle of with his "Desert Island" discs. As nostalgic as the shop, so is the subtle carrier bag, like the product, "a stimulus to the imagination."

London, Paris, New York, Tokyo, and Milan. →

Elizabeth Arden
Red Door Salon & Spa

Q. What's behind that red door?
A. Some of the most stylish women in the world. Open the door to true pampering from head to toe. If you can't squeeze a vacation into your hectic schedule, then take a few hours (or even a full day) at the Red Door and live Elizabeth Arden's beauty dream. Leave those cares behind by paying others to care for you. And, once you've finished, you leave with your hands (carefully) carrying the Red Door shopping bag, filled with all the necessities to keep the beauty-dream going.

Wherever a Red Door beckons. Also at Saks Fifth Avenue, where the beauty salon has metamorphosized into a . . . Red Door. →

The Jewel Box is housed in the first Elizabeth Arden building outside of New York City in Washington, D.C. To honor this landmark building, the three-generation family-owned jewelry store added a picture of the building on the shopping bag and subtly placed the name of the store above the door so as not to compete with the architectural image.

BAGTOID

IT WAS ONLY A MATTER OF TIME BEFORE THE WORLD'S CAPITALISTIC CAPITAL
WOULD FIND A WAY TO GET PEOPLE TO SHOP MORE.
BY LINKING SHOPS TOGETHER THAT WOULD BE IMPERVIOUS TO THE WEATHER.
WHEN THE FIRST CLIMATE CONTROL MALL WENT UP IN 1956
(SOUTHDALE, JUST OUTSIDE OF MINNEAPOLIS—WHAT IS IT ABOUT MINNESOTA AND SHOPPING?),
THERE WAS NO TURNING BACK.
SOON PEOPLE WERE GOING TO MALLS FOR ALL THEIR NEEDS, AND KIDS FOUND A NEW PLACE TO HANG.
NOW THE MALL HAS BECOME A CENTER OF LIVING.
EVERY TIME A NEW ONE GOES UP, MORE AND MORE SMALL STORES AND MAIN STREETS CLOSE.
ON AUGUST 11, 1992, THE MALL OF AMERICA—
THE MOTHER OF ALL MALLS—OPENED IN BLOOMINGTON, MINNESOTA, AND RECORDED A MAJOR VICTORY FOR

THE MALLING OF AMERICA

• More than 1,500 couples have gotten married at Mall of America's Chapel of Love • More than 500 stores • The most visited destination for U.S. travelers • More visitors annually than Disney World, Graceland, and the Grand Canyon combined • Voted best shopping destination in the U.S. • More than 200 million visits have been made to Mall of America since its opening August 11, 1992, through 1997 • Attracts more than 42.5 million visitors per year • Tourism from outside a 150 mile radius accounts for more than 37 percent of all traffic • International visitors account for approximately six percent or nearly 2.6 million of the Mall's annual traffic • The three leading countries for international tourists are Canada, Japan, and the UK • Since its opening, more than 60,000 organized tour groups have visited the Mall • More than 4,000 people have hunted their way through Mall of America as part of organized scavenger hunts by the Mall's tourism department • 600,000 to 900,000 people visit the Mall per week • It cost more than $650 million to build • It encompasses 4.2 million square feet • 22 sit-down restaurants • 27 fast food restaurants • 34 specialty food stores • 8 nightclubs • 14 theater screens • Brings in $1.5 billion annually to Minnesota • 11,000 year-round employees • 13,000 employees during summers and holidays • 12,750 parking spaces on site; 7,000 off-site • Key attractions: Knott's Camp Snoopy, UnderWater World, LEGOR Imagination Center, Golf Mountain •Walking distance around one level of Mall of America is 0.57 miles • Total store front footage is 4.3 miles • If a shopper spent ten minutes browsing at every store it would take more than 86 hours to complete their visit • 258 Statue of Liberty's could lay inside the Mall • 67 Washington Monuments could lay inside the Mall • If Mall of America had a retractable roof, nine Eiffel Towers could stand inside • If Mount Rushmore was divided into individual monuments, a president could reside in each of the Mall's four courts • Mall of America's 4.2 million square feet would hold 24,336 buses • More than 45 miles of US West phone lines are strung throughout the Mall • Mall of America is big enough to hold 32 Boeing 747s • More than 25 million rides have been given at Knott's Camp Snoopy in its first five years • More than 3,000 individuals are registered in the "Mall Walker" program. (The 1996 Mall Walker of the Year walked off 140 pounds) • Mall of America has its own weekly newspaper, *Best of the Mall* • In its first five years, the Mall generated 34,700 tons of waste • 44 escalators and 17 elevators • One phone number for mall information 612–883–8800 • There is no sales tax on clothing in Minnesota • National American University is the first-ever college campus in a mall • It's a mall world, after all •

WHILE MOST PEOPLE ARE WORRIED ABOUT
THE APPROACH OF THE YEAR 2000,
WE CAN'T HELP BUT WONDER HOW THE SHOPPING BAG WILL FARE . . .

WAY BEYOND THE MILLENNIUM
HERE ARE SOME THOUGHTS FROM THE EXPERTS:

"The shopping bag is clearly a useful form. I am always saving my bags and reusing them. However, at any given time, I inevitably have many more bags than I will ever reuse. I worry about throwing them away and continue to hoard them. Therefore, as a vision for the next millennium shopping bag, I hope that the bags will diminish in quantity, but improve in quality and durability. We might be more likely to mend our wasteful, disposable habits with fewer, better bags, that will ask to be saved and reused. They can have great shapes, colors, and graphics, and I expect that they will be made of new and amazing materials that will be stronger and more lasting. Or, perhaps they will self-destruct after a given time in an environmentally friendly way! A 'use-or-lose' concept!"
Dorothy Twining Globus, Director, The Museum at the Fashion Institute of Technology

"With ever-increasing on-line shopping, I see an antistatic shopping bag with multiple gussets and pop-up handles that take it from flatter and mailable to fatter and carryable, and the ubiquitous shopping bag morphs into: the CYBERBAG. . . ."
Susan Slover, Director, slover [AND] company

"From box to bag it has evolved
in different shape and size
paper, plastic, fabric, board
anything you can devise

Printed, stamped, embossed, or screened
most anything can be done
draw an image and sketch it out
that is most of the fun

The future of the shopping bag
is unlimited, as can be
with new materials on the market
that no one can foresee

Everyone carries some kind of tote
to hold books, lunch, and things
the Millennium will see exciting shapes
as we may have bags with wings."

Joyce Mintzer, Executive Vice President, S. Posner Sons, Inc.

"Shopping Bags of tomorrow? Will they exist at all as we know them? I imagine them in new materials, reusable and recyclable, in new forms produced by new technology. Fun and exciting."
Ivan Chermayeff, Chermayeff & Geismar, Inc.

"Instant and free!"
Alex Lindsay, President, ModernArts Packaging, Inc.

Right: Millennium
bag designed by
Alex Lindsay

INDEX